No Blushes
Renju Renjimar

ALT *life* — voices and stories

AltLife offers stories of individuals, communities and societies. Their voices bear witness to a history, a milieu, an experience, and offer new ways of seeing and understanding our times.

No Blushes
Renju Renjimar

as told to
Sonya J. Nair

Orient BlackSwan

All rights reserved. No part of this book may be (i) modified, reproduced or utilised in any form, or by any means, electronic or mechanical, including photocopying, recording or by any information storage and retrieval system, in any form of binding or cover other than in which it is published, without permission in writing from the publisher; or (ii) used or reproduced in any manner for the purpose of training, development or operation of artificial intelligence (AI) technologies and systems, including generative AI technologies, without permission in writing from the copyright holder.

NO BLUSHES: RENJU RENJIMAR

ORIENT BLACKSWAN PRIVATE LIMITED

Registered Office
3-6-752 Himayatnagar, Hyderabad 500 029, Telangana, India
Email: centraloffice@orientblackswan.com

Other Offices
Bengaluru, Chennai, Guwahati, Hyderabad, Kolkata, Mumbai, New Delhi, Noida, Patna

© Orient Blackswan Private Limited 2026
First published 2026

ISBN 978 93 6973 049 0

Typeset in Cambria 13/15 *by*
K. Divya, Hyderabad 500 060

Printed at
Manipal Technologies Limited, Manipal

Published by
Orient Blackswan Private Limited
3-6-752, Himayatnagar,
Hyderabad 500 029, Telangana, India
Email: info@orientblackswan.com

041732

This book is dedicated

to my mother, to my family—of blood and of bonds formed over time—my friends and daughters from the community and from the entertainment industry, to all the people who have helped me, to all those who have walked away, to those I loved and lost, to all the people in the real and virtual worlds who have looked out for me, to the tears and the joys of my community, to the eternal Goddess from whom nothing stays hidden.

—**Renju Renjimar**

to Renju, a vault of patience and a precious person, to my family, to my friends, especially Kukku Xavier without whom the world would have been too much for me, to Samra Fuad who saw the typos I made but still respects me, to Soni Somarajan who is the dearest of dears, to G. S. Jayasree and Sreedevi K. Nair of Samyukta Research Foundation whose faith in me is both touching and puzzling, to my father Jayakumar V. who is no more and who is missed every single day, to my mother Yeshoda Nair who taught me all that I know and all that I am learning, to Yellamma—with whom it all began . . .

—**Sonya J. Nair**

Contents

Preface	ix
Chapter One	1
Chapter Two	23
Chapter Three	35
Chapter Four	47
Chapter Five	59
Chapter Six	71
Chapter Seven	81

Preface

I first met Renju Renjimar when she came to All Saints' College, Thiruvananthapuram, Kerala, in 2018. I was working in the English Department and was in charge of the Equal Opportunities Cell. I was also working on my doctoral thesis on transgender festivals of South India. She was leading a group from Dhwayah and was visiting the college to perform for the students. This was the first time transpeople had ever entered this college, and the students were really excited to see and listen to the great Renju Renjimar and other trans-activists.

We got talking, Renju and I, and I did not feel like I was talking with a stranger. There was nothing profound in our conversation—just everyday, desultory things. But there was a level of comfort. I looked at her and saw an honest, driven, committed person who wore her fame lightly. She flitted from performer to performer, applying deft touches of makeup and talking away nineteen to the dozen. She put everyone at ease. They all deferred to her; when she spoke, they listened.

Finally, it was time for Dhwayah to perform. Ananyah, who you will meet in these pages, was their emcee. The speakers included Sheethal Shyam, one of the most visible faces of the trans community in Kerala, and Shyama S. Prabha, the community's hope for a civil servant amongst them. They put up an electrifying performance. The energy remained with the audience for days to come.

As all this glitz and energy exploded onto the college stage, I turned to Renju and said, 'I would like to write your story. What do you think?'

She laughed aloud and said, 'Ma'am, many people have approached me for my story, but I did not want to commit to them. I felt that they would exploit me or that they would not say the truths that I want to say. But you, I feel differently about though we have only just met. I agree. Let us do it!'

Thus began an association that has lasted nearly a decade. I began to meet Renju frequently, either I would go to Ernakulam where she has her base, or she would come down to Thiruvananthapuram and we would talk. Over a series of conversations, I understood the person I was going to write about. I understood her desires and dreams. I also observed how the trajectory of her life unfurled and blossomed.

One might wonder why it took me the better part of a decade to write about an individual's life. That is just the way it is. Renju's life was not just a task or assignment for me. Her life had to mean something for those reading about her. And for that, I had to grow as a person as well. I had to understand how the many, many things I took for granted as a woman, or even got irritated with as a woman, held immense fascination and significance for Renju. I had to understand that while I used to weigh the pros and cons of being a woman in a patriarchal society, here was someone who had to visualise an added dimension to her life in the same society. Slowly and steadily, I grew to discern, to think and to express.

What makes someone spill their life to a stranger? Would they be keeping anything back? Are there things they are not telling? These suspicions often traversed my mind, just as they will run through your mind when you read any biography. But then, someone with the courage to live her truth under the harshest of glares, someone with the sense of responsibility to extend a helping hand to those struggling, will speak only the truth. In any case, this is the story that Renju Renjimar chooses to tell. And it is a compelling tale.

As I finally sat down to write this life, I thought of the *Mahabharata*. When the sage Veda Vyasa wanted to get the epic written down, Lord Ganesha agreed to be his scribe provided the sage did not pause at any point in his narration. The canny Vyasa in turn told Ganesha that he must fully understand the import of the verses he was writing down. I have understood Renju. And thus begins her saga, as told to, and by, me.

Sonya J. Nair

Chapter One

My earliest memory is of stealing my aunt's artificial hair bun, planting it on my head and prancing around. I was fascinated by that hair bun. Feeling that softness between my fingers and the way it sat on my head—it made me very happy. I was five. And I was a boy. But no one in my family minded. They thought it was great fun and it was, after all, a little kid amusing himself and entertaining others. They were mistaken. In my young mind, I was churning out dreams and fantasies—of luxuriant hair, oiled and plaited, hanging down my back. I would flick it at imaginary people who were fascinated by how beautiful I looked with all that hair. I would place that bun atop my head like a pineapple and walk around pretending to be sophisticated—whatever my interpretation was of sophistication at that age. I was a ticking time bomb and no one knew.

Born in 1974, I was the fourth child of Thankamma and Thankappan, whose names meant 'Golden Woman' and 'Golden Man'. This delightful mix of coincidence and irony never ceased to tickle me. There was nothing golden about us materially, but we were happy in our own way. We lived in the little village of Punthalathazham in the Kollam district of Kerala where paddy fields abounded and there was no dearth of blue skies or clean air. The members of our extended family did not stray too far and we all lived in a cluster of houses within shouting distance of each other. This was both a blessing and a curse. A blessing because everyone was always in the know of things and would volunteer to look after you or come help you out. All celebrations were like mini-festivals and actual festivals were like local events. We all had a grand time with the little that we had. It was the village version of living it up. A curse because everyone knew everything and there were ten people to take you to task if you were naughty.

On Onam and Vishu—the two festivals of Kerala—one marking the harvest season and the other celebrating the solstice, we used to be bought new clothes. I was never happy with mine. Mostly I would wear my brothers' hand-me-downs. That was bad enough as I would imagine the wear and tear that these clothes had undergone because my brothers were always rolling on the ground, wrestling or playing some game that involved running around. And for festivals, I was stuffed into new shirts and shorts. It was galling, to say the least. I would see girls playing in their frocks or skirts and longed to have these dresses. To be able walk with skirts swishing around my legs was like an unattainable dream. Till I told myself it need not be so. At our local temple, the devi, Goddess Bhagavathy, is the deity. Every year we have an *Ulsavam*—a festival in her honour—at the Peroorkavu temple. Bhagavathy comes out of the temple to survey her people, to bring prosperity and cure disease. The young children of the village dress up and stand on either side of the path carrying trays containing *diya*s, flowers and incense sticks to welcome her. My aunt had pledged that I too would carry the lamp. I was over the moon.

The euphoria lasted till I realised I was meant to be dressed as I usually was. I was extremely angry and threw an almighty tantrum. I stubbornly refused to listen to entreaties or bow down to threats. And there is not much you can do to a child of five. My poor aunt relented. I knew she had to. You do not break a promise you made to the goddess! She borrowed a frock from a neighbour and that was how, for the first time, I was able to breathe in my skin. Standing there amidst all the chattering girls and their mothers, I felt at home for the first time. I did not have that unsettling feeling that something was wrong with me and that I must hide this dangerous secret. No. I wanted to crow from the rooftops, 'This is me . . . look at me!' The goddess arrived, looking resplendent atop an elephant. I felt that she was looking directly at me and that she loved me. I became her devotee for life.

When I was not decked up in festival finery, I was a scrawny boy with long limbs and a soulful face. I had huge eyes that took up most of my face and I used to wonder when I would grow into them. There was never any awkwardness or gawkiness one associates with young boys. I think that was because I was not a boy and have never have been one. My sister, Ajitha Kumari, was the eldest, followed by my two brothers Raju and Rajendran. I was . . . well, who I was is irrelevant, so never mind. The four of us grew up together in a little house that was built and maintained by our hardworking parents. My mother worked in the nearby cashew nut factory, and my father was a daily-wage labourer. Our income was never fixed or secure, but we made do. My sister stopped going to school after the tenth standard. The rest of us were made to go to school. My brothers were rather indifferent students, yet they were doggedly sent to school by my parents. I was quite a good student with very orderly and neat handwriting. My parents saw education as a way of getting out of the rut of economic insecurity. My mother used to come back after long hours of processing the cashew nuts. Those costly nuts went halfway across the world yet those handling them were ill-paid and overworked. My father did back-breaking work day after day in the fields or on construction sites. There was no such thing as taking a day off or lying in; time was literally money in our house.

Standing in the front yard of my house, I could see acres of paddy fields. These fields never ceased to amaze me. Much of my childhood was centred around them. In the monsoons, the fields would flood and become mini ponds in which we splashed around. When the young paddy grains pushed through we would munch on them, feeling the wooden taste flooding our mouths. In the height of summer, these fields would develop cracks and we would peer into the heart of the earth. This was my world for a long time—the fields, the temple, the goddess in it, the games we played, boys football and girls hopscotch. I naturally wanted to join the girls but they wouldn't take me in and the boys would not let me get away. Sometimes I just watched days passing me by. Life was serene and beautiful.

I was extremely attached to my mother and would not leave her side for a minute if I could help it. After two boys, my mother yearned for a girl. She did have my sister, but that was years ago. In fact, everyone in our family thought I would be a girl. So imagine the disappointment when I arrived bawling—a boy! But my mother would often line my eyes and draw over my eyebrows with kohl and say I looked adorable. And I believed her. Once home from school, I would be stuck to my mother's side. In our area, when women had their periods, they would stay in an outhouse and not come in till the period was done. Those four or five days would be unbearable for me as I would not get to sleep next to my mother. Finally, one day, I declared that I too had periods and went off to be with my mother. I did not enter the house till her days were done. My poor sister had to lug bathing water to the yard not only for my mother but also for me. This soon became a practice that no one thought of as odd. Everyone just played along, I suppose, indulgently thinking that I would grow out of it.

My mother was, I guess, flattered that at least one of her sons was emotionally available. She loved me dearly and rarely said a harsh word to me. There were times when, lying next to her, I wanted to blurt out about how I felt—that her wish had come true and that within me was her daughter. There were no secrets between my mother and myself. But something held me back. I used to console myself thinking that the time hadn't come for me talk about it.

I had three best friends in the village, Unni, Mohan and Nawaz or, as they called themselves, Unniamma, Mohini and Jumairath. We all felt trapped in the wrong body and would never lose an opportunity to dress up. Our grand day of getting decked up was the temple festival, when the whole village and neighbouring areas would gather for the festivities, the fair and the annual play. We would all line our eyes, paint our nails, apply tons of powder, wear neatly pressed clothes and stand around looking shy. I still remember our racoon-like faces in the garish yellow light emanating from the stage where the play was being performed. We thought we looked beautiful. God knows how funny we actually looked.

We were not persecuted or humiliated by others. We were generally treated well. At school, however, I had torrid experiences in the early years. I used to insist that I wanted to wear frocks to Lakshmi Vilasam School where I was enrolled, and such was my adamant nature that my parents allowed it. My classmates had a field day taunting me. This caused me great anguish and confusion as I really did not understand what was happening. I was just a kid, four years or so of age. My parents consulted my teacher, Kunjamma Saar as we called her, and she said, 'Let the child do whatever he wants to. All the criticism will soon die down.' That's what happened. I turned up day after day in frocks and soon the kids lost interest in taunting me. After the initial months, I started turning up in the boys' uniform and soon everyone forgot all about those days. Except me, of course. In later years, my classmates did not taunt me for being effeminate. I suppose these were all contributing factors that led me to grow up confident in my identity. I fell in love for the first time when I was in the ninth standard. He was a goldsmith—there is the gold connection again! He was a handsome man, quite a bit older than I was. He would be standing by the gate when I passed by on my way to school. His house was quite close to mine and we knew each other by sight. He occupied my dreams and my waking hours. Every film song was about him, every romantic scene featured both of us. I recorded the tempestuous feelings of my love for him in my diary and even scripted how our life together would be. Soon, my one-sided love reached a fever pitch. It refused to be contained. It demanded answers. So, armed with a letter, I went up to him and handed it over. The minute he took the letter from me, I knew something was wrong, that I had made a mistake. Then I thought, as Lata Mangeshkar sang, *'Pyar kiya toh darna kya?'* (Why be afraid if you are in love?) and continued on my way to school.

The answer to Lata *didi*'s question awaited me in the evening when I returned home from school. The entire extended family was assembled in front of my house. Normally people do that only if someone has died. Heart thudding, I ran in and counted my family. They all seemed to be alive. It was only when I saw the letter in my sister's hand that I realised it was I who was going to die. That man had come straight to my home and handed the letter over to my people. He could not have rebuffed me more thoroughly. I thought I was done for. And there was my sister reading aloud from my diary—my little narratives of love were met with sniggers. My confessions, desires somehow seemed soiled or dirty when she read them in her slightly mocking voice. In the end, I was asked not to do such stupid things like giving letters to men. They chided me for not knowing that I should be writing love letters to girls. Even today when I think of that man, I am annoyed. I still think it was a terrible thing that he did.

The next year passed without incident. In the vacation that followed my tenth-standard exams, I went to work in the nearby brick kiln. I was a hard worker and was quite popular there. The money I earned would almost entirely go towards household expenses. I say almost because I would use a little bit to buy nail polish, kohl and other little things. A girl had to look good! The summer went by, my results came and I had passed. I joined Fatima Mata National College in Kollam for my pre-degree. I would attend tuition classes for some subjects, Malayalam being one of them. That is where I fell in love again, this time with my Malayalam teacher. I used to watch him day after day, standing in front of the class, reciting poems or reading out sections of novels in his deep voice. I would get goosebumps when he asked me questions and I would reply bashfully. When he came around to check our work, my heart would start beating wildly. He had no inkling of the way I felt about him. Yet again, I decided to express my feelings through a letter. This time, I decided to be discreet. None of my earlier tactics of being bold and upfront. The classes had partitions made of thatched, dried coconut fronds. One could make a small hole and see and listen to what was happening in the next class. I decided to pass him the letter through such an opening. He only saw a hand with manicured nails stretching out a letter towards him. I think he automatically took the letter and then walked on. I suppose he was used to getting letters from female students all the time. I had not written my name in the letter so I do not know now how he was supposed to guess it was me. I suppose I thought he would hear my heart calling out to him! But the discovery came in a staider fashion.

On his usual rounds checking the work of students, he came to my desk and bent over and froze. Then without saying a word, he moved on to other students. I realised he had noticed the distinct nail polish on my nails and understood it wasn't a princess but a prince who was in love with him. Since then, he began to assiduously avoid me. I understand that people do not have to reciprocate one's feelings, but they do not have to avoid one. It was not like I was going to jump out at him from some dark corner. Or perhaps that was what he thought I might do. It is, after all, one of the fundamental arguments that homophobes make. The thing was that my attraction did not strike me as a homosexual one. Because in my mind I was a woman. Anyway, it did not matter to me as even then, as a child, 'no' meant just that—no. I did, however, wish things had not become so awkward between us.

But love did come to me in the most unexpected of places—in the pay ward of a government hospital. My friend was admitted there and I was the designated bystander. There was one other occupant in the room but he was on the other side of a cloth partition. In the evenings, when visitors were allowed, my other friends would join us and we would chatter away endlessly. Sometimes I would break into a song-and-dance routine and entertain them all. Unknown to us, the other occupant was witnessing all this silently. One day, the curtain parted and a young man, slightly older than I, peered out. I was not at all annoyed. It was a good-natured face, one that was capable of being amused easily. He had bright eyes and lovely hair. I just liked him. The thought of this possibly heading anywhere never crossed my mind. I was, after all, reeling from my earlier rejection. 'What's your name?' he asked. I told him.

'That's a good name. I am M–' I smiled in reply. 'You dance really well, I sometimes watch you.' I could only blush at his referring to my antics as 'dance'. 'Oh well, it is nothing, really . . .' I trailed off.

Then we began to include him in our conversations. On some afternoons, when my friend dozed off, I would go sit with M. We talked about our homes, our families, what we wanted out of life—juvenile things, really. I understood that he belonged to a prominent family in Kollam. Their social standing was way above ours. His brother was a doctor, leading M to have special privileges in the hospital; and with the nurses checking in on him frequently, he did not really need a bystander. This was fine by him as he preferred being by himself. We were as different as chalk and cheese in terms of our background, education and upbringing. But what we both did have in common was a need to be accepted as we were. I would perch on the edge of his bed and talk of all kinds of things while he listened with a smile. During one conversation, I realised that our fingers were intertwined. I stopped mid-sentence and swallowed hard. Words failed me. This was the first time that someone had touched me like that, with love, with desire, with acceptance. The silence of that hospital room resounded with the whispers of our love.

I think I resented my friend for getting better and being discharged from the hospital! But soon, M was fine too. We would meet at designated times and locations as landlines were not common and mobile phones were not even invented then, I think. Time would just fly in his company. We made such grand plans of what we would do in life and how we would pamper each other. We were young and in love. The idea of a yawning abyss did not exist in our lives.

My student life ended abruptly with the sudden death of my father. He had a heart attack and was gone—just like that. I was not with him when it happened and when

I did get home as usual, I once again found the yard full of people. I jokingly wondered if it was the replay of my old letter incident, but then I heard the wailing from the house. I rushed in to find my father laid out and people preparing for the rites. My Golden Man was leaving us and I was trying to recall the last thing I had said to him. Nothing came to mind. It was like a shroud had been draped over my memories too.

Father was gone and after the mourning period was over, everyone else left too. I did not want to stay there anymore. My sister had been married, and debts incurred in connection with the wedding had to be repaid. My brothers were not very happy about parting with their earnings, and it hurt me to see my mother think of taking on extra work after her day at the cashew factory. I asked my friends to help and one of them found me a job at a school hostel in the nearby district of Pathanamthitta. It was hard work, but they would provide free food and accommodation. So, my salary was essentially my savings. I decided to take it up despite my mother's entreaties to continue my studies.

M reached out to me and offered to help me however he could. I was just happy that he was still willing to stand by me. With the memory of my mother's tearful face and M's words in my ears, I set off to manage the hostel—cook, clean, get the students out on time, look after their clothes and tend to their illnesses and scrapes; in short, be the whole and soul of the place. The pay was not much, but it was food on the table and helped pay a good part of our debt.

I would probably have just gone on like that if it were not for the impending Onam vacation. The hostel was closing so I called M to fix a day to meet him. He asked me over to his place and I readily agreed. On the appointed day I set out from home, took the bus and reached his place. His mother informed me that his friends had arrived and he had headed out to watch a movie with them. I was put out. We were meeting after such a long time and I was there on his invitation. Extremely irritated, I went to the theatre complex, bought a ticket for another movie playing there and settled down to watch it. The movie had begun ages ago, but I did not care. I just wanted to prove to him that I too knew how to have a good time and did not need him. When the movie ended, I walked by the lobby where I heard some people talking of a scuffle that had broken out in the other theatre. I was too angry to listen any further and headed home, determined not to be the first one to initiate any contact with M. It was a lover's tiff in my mind, and he had to set it right. The vacation came to a close with no word from M. I returned to the hostel. But how long can one remain annoyed with the love of one's life? On a long weekend I went home and took off straight to M's house. His mother answered the doorbell. I was shocked to see her dishevelled appearance. There were dark circles around her eyes and she began weeping when she saw me.

    I looked past her and saw on the wall straight ahead—his photograph with a string of flowers hanging around it. Dead? How could he be dead? We had planned an entire life together. There was so much that we had to do. It was only on that one day that I tried to show him that I could live without him. I hadn't meant it, anyway. That didn't mean he could just go away and leave me to fend for myself. I returned to earth to hear his mother tell me that the day I had gone looking for him, he was watching a film, and a scuffle had broken out in the theatre and he had been stabbed. They rushed him to the local hospital for emergency care and then to Trivandrum Medical College, where he had been admitted for fourteen days. He had died on the fifteenth day. My love breathed its last, just as it had begun, in a hospital.

On the way home, I kept thinking of those two weeks—would he have thought of me at least once? Would he have wished I were there by his side? Worst of all, if I had been there and had sung and danced for him and held his hand, would he have survived? He might have been hurt and upset that I did not go looking for him all those days that he was in hospital. He will never know how much I missed him and that I was sorry I did not find out about him. I wanted to apologise for my petulance. But he was long gone. Not even his ashes remained. Unless... and then the idea began to take root in my mind. Unless I joined him. He would be happy that I went to meet him. We could still be together. I felt happy. Light. Like he was sitting next to me and this was what he wanted. I went home and, without any final words to anyone, consumed poison. But maybe this was not what M had wanted because I opened my eyes to the sight of my weeping mother. My brothers were sullenly silent: perhaps they were told by my mother not to say anything.

I was discharged after twenty-one days. My mother did not castigate me for my selfishness, nor did anyone ask why I had taken such a drastic step. The family felt it was best I looked for work nearby. I resigned from the school and went back to working in the brick kiln. Then I switched to working in a saw mill. While the men worked bare-chested, I would be wearing a full-sleeved shirt and a lungi that I would never lift above my knees. I maintained my modesty like the women who worked there. Some of my best friends there were women. The men too did not mind me. I was healing slowly. But I suppose, like the children of God, I too had the great desert to cross in search of my true destiny. My story was just beginning.

In our society, ignorance—whether genuine or feigned—is seen as bliss. The 'don't ask, don't tell policy' is not exclusive to the US army. It is universal in its application and implications. So long as I did not peel back my family's eyelids and force them to take a look at my gradually surfacing reality, they were fine. My walking around with painted nails or being discovered wearing my mother's saree were all seen as playacting, childishness, pranks and so on. But I was a child no more and it was becoming impossible to ignore the statement I was making. I suppose this got one of my brothers riled up and he barged into the house to take me to task. I suppose it could have been a crass remark passed by his mates or the fact that my mother was being so indulgent towards a son who was so clearly a deviant. My brothers used to resent the bond between us. It did not matter that it was just the both of us who were working off the financial burden and preventing our home from falling into the hands of the debt collectors.

My brother rushed into the room and began raining blows on me. I tried to fend him off. It started to really hurt and I found blood trickling down my nose. This provoked me and I began to hit him back. He finally gave me an almighty shove and walked out, yelling that he would come back later and show me how dangerous he really could be. I decided that I had had enough. I couldn't handle such hostility and violence. I packed up a few of my things and went to meet my mother at the factory. She came to the gate which was locked and would not open till it was closing time. I narrated everything to her and took her leave. She began pleading with me to stay till she got off work so she could do something. I refused. I was afraid that if she talked to me, my resolve would weaken and I would stay back. But I had to get out of that mire. I wanted to explore the world and strike out on my own. I had begun feeling that there was another life waiting for me.

My friend had arranged employment for me at the house of the sister of Abubakar Abdul Rahim, the Honourable Former Governor of Meghalaya. It was a huge house where the matriarch presided over the lives of her three boys and four girls. They were kind people who treated me very gently. But what held me there was the little boy of Noushad, one of the sons. He was about three and his mother had passed away. He readily took to me. I used to look after him as his mother would have. Being with that child brought to the surface all the hopes I had of being the woman that I knew myself to be deep within. The compulsion was too strong to ignore. I realised that being stuck in small towns doing household chores would bind me to a life of menial jobs. I would not get anywhere. This made me want to move to a bigger city where there would be better opportunities.

This was why, when an acquaintance mentioned an opening for a servant in Advocate T. V. Prabhakar's house, I grabbed the chance. The money was good and they also promised to help me study further. I boarded a truck for the first time in my life and reached Ernakulam. The city was so alive. There was so much happening. Thanks to the port and the naval base, there was a diverse demographic. There were people who spoke Tulu, Gujarati, Tamil, Hindi and a number of other languages. The cultural confluence made the place vibrant. I revelled in the air of Fort Kochi and would gaze at the sea for hours together. I was anonymous in Ernakulam. No one cared who I was or how I wanted to present my identity. There simply was no time to bother. But I was afraid of revealing my true self anywhere. I would just play out my fantasies in my head.

Contrary to what was promised me, no steps were taken to get me an education. Each day was the same, except on the select days that I was allowed to have some time off. I would finish all the work and then retire to the space allotted to me. It would be late night by then. Yet that was when my day truly came alive. I would line my eyes with kohl, dress in clothes of my choice and twirl around. It was my private world. But I was not happy. This sneaking around was bothering me. I felt like a caged bird. The servant in one of the houses on our lane also harboured the same secrets as I did. She then introduced me to other members of our community. It was so liberating to have some company. They encouraged me to quit my job and join them. I agreed. This marked yet another turning point in my life.

In the early 1990s, members of the gay and transgender community were clubbed under the category 'MSM' (Men who Have Sex with Men). Most of the activities of the NGOs established for the uplift of the community were concerned with the prevention of sexually transmitted diseases, mainly AIDS. The solution that they found for the same was to distribute condoms. This was what we were also employed to do. We were part of Shrama, the Cochin branch of the Sahodaran Foundation. We would distribute contraceptives amongst our community members and sex workers and keep track of the various awareness programmes that the organisation conducted. I made friends with the members I was sent out with. They were an interesting set of people, always whispering and laughing. I was enchanted. I had never been among people like me. It was a whole new experience.

One day, my friends took me to a textile shop. We were looking through the various racks and discussing what suited us best. I liked a saree and bought it. I collected my purchase and stepped out of the shop with my friends when one of the salespersons yelled, 'Thief.' I stopped and turned around to look for the thief. There was no one. The people in the shop surrounded me. I was taken aback and looked to my friends for support and was astonished to find them running away. The shop people handed me over to the police. I showed the police the bill of the dress that I had purchased. The police too understood that I was innocent and had no grounds on which to arrest me. But still, I was taken into custody and remanded for a week. By the second day in jail, I became familiar with the inmates. We were all friends there and I was secure. Still, being incarcerated was hurtful. I did not know what to do or what my future would be. I had called my people at home and asked them to arrange for my bail. By the seventh day, I was thoroughly depressed. I raised my hands and appealed to St Antony at Kaloor Church in Kochi. I don't know if you will believe me, but this is the truth—I saw St Antony in my palms. It was cathartic. Almost immediately, a policeman came and informed me that my bail had been posted. I was released. My case was eventually dismissed.

It was a decisive point in my life. I renewed my resolve that I would never ever get on the wrong side of the law. I teamed up with a friend and began going door to door selling books. It was never easy getting people to open doors to allow me to display my books at their doorstep. But I managed it. I would ask them for food, if they had any to spare, and they would invariably feed me too. I was not ashamed to ask for help. It only made me even more determined to reach self-sufficiency and strive for dignity. It was at this point that I made friends with another member of the community; his birth name was Sudhakaran. He offered me a place to stay. We began helping out at his sister's roadside eatery. Our job was to make dosas and serve the customers. We were paid fifty rupees per day and food was free. I was considered auspicious by the brother-sister duo as their business tripled after I began working there. This irritated the owners of the nearby stalls and, one night, they send hired goons to attack us. I was severely injured. But that only made me more determined to work harder. I suppose hell hath no fury like a woman angered; I was, after all, not scorned!

I had re-established contact with my family while at Noushad's house and regularly sent money home. But often I was kept out of family functions by my brother who had attacked me. In fact, it was only during one of my weekly phone calls that I came to know that his wedding had already taken place. It hurt me no end, but I took it in my stride. I had promised myself that I would not be disheartened no matter what the hurdle. What kept me going during all those dark days was my unshakeable faith in the Goddess Sree Devi, the reigning deity of the Kottankulangara temple in Kollam. This temple is unlike any other in Kerala, both in its origin stories and in the rituals observed there.

It is said that a long, long time ago there was a group of cowherds, young boys, who were playing in the nearby woods. They hit a coconut against a stone to de-husk it. The stone began to bleed. The frightened boys ran to the village elders and priests, who divined the presence of Vana Durga and decreed that a temple be built on the spot. Being the goddess of the forest, her spirit needed to roam free and she had to remain in constant sight of the open sky, as her energy must never be contained in a closed space. Hence, the sanctum sanctorum had no roof. The goddess wished that the cowherd boys carry the ceremonial plates heralding her arrival into the temple. As the *thalapoli* is meant to be carried only by girls, the boys dressed as girls and stood ready to welcome the goddess.

Since then, men began dressing as women and holding the ceremonial lamps for the goddess as a gesture of gratitude for fulfilling the appeals that they had made to her. Sometimes whole families pray to the goddess and when she grants their prayers, the man of the house dresses up as a woman and holds the lamp. The festival takes place every year on the tenth and eleventh days of the Malayalam month of *Meenam* (March). The festival is called the *Chamayavilakku* (*chamayam* meaning, 'makeup' or 'adornments' and *vilakku*, meaning 'lamp'), referring to the practice of men donning female attire to please the goddess. I was about thirteen when I first went for the festival. I was in awe. It was not just the sheer opulence of the participants that impressed me—the men all looked like voluptuous women, well dressed and decked out in ornaments—it was the sheer power emanating from the goddess. It was a source of never-ending benevolence and energy. She set out on her elephant to survey her people and when she returned in the wee hours of the morning, her subjects awaited her, lighting the way. I saw devotion, admiration and pure bliss. Amidst the rhythm of the drums and the cymbals and the lit lamps, I gazed at the goddess and prayed with all the fervour I was capable of. I begged her to make me a woman. When I went home, I felt like I was carrying a part of her power back with me. Since then, I have never missed the festival even for a single year. I had a gold ring that I would pawn every year to arrange to pay for the festival finery. I would redeem it after a few days. This cycle continued till the goddess blessed me with the means of going to her in a state of prosperity. No matter what the work is, if it clashes with the festival, I simply decline. But with the passing years, I have modified my prayers. I now pray that she helps me remain who I am. I am happy and at peace with myself.

It was for this festival that I began training myself in the nuances of makeup. My friends in the village were all very competitive when it came to dressing up for the festival. One need not be a Hindu; many from other parts of the country as well as foreigners too come to participate. My friends and I would keep our dresses a big secret. We all would accessorise with the utmost care and it was out of the question to lend someone even a safety pin, lest they end up looking better! I began to study pictures of models in order to understand the techniques that were employed for their makeup. Finally, I would try it out on myself and my friends with varying degrees of success. Over time, I learned to investigate the finer points such as skin tone and definition. These days, I am often asked for tips on makeup and my constant advice is to never overdo it. You must identify your outstanding feature or select the feature that you wish to highlight and then get to work on it. Let your personality show through. Even neon makeup can look wonderful if you have the personality for it! That is why I really admire Lady Gaga—she is fearless and she shows it.

Between selling books and working at the food stall, I met R. L. B. Unnikrishnan, an artist and teacher and someone whom I consider my mentor. He gave me opportunities that helped me start off in life. I began doing the makeup for his students' stage performances. They began to win prizes in various district- and state-level competitions. I was seen as a lucky charm. I found my popularity rising. Soon a friend helped me find work on the sets of a film where I did the makeup for junior artists. Gradually, I began working with leading artists in the Malayalam film industry. All this did not happen overnight. The climb was slow, filled with tears, humiliation and hard work. Just like the trajectory of my transformation.

I decided that unless I was true to myself, I would not find peace. So, I began to slowly change myself. I began wearing long kurtas, grew out my hair, my nails were always painted and I began shaping my eyebrows. All this raised quite some eyebrows. To all queries I replied, with a smile and equanimity, 'This is who I am.' I began to discern changes in the people around me which were directly proportional to the changes I had brought about in myself. I found myself being sidelined and discriminated against. Tea would be served on the sets and those around me would all get their cup. When I asked for a cup, I would be told to wait. Finally, my designated artist would have to ask on my behalf and the tea would appear in an instant. The irony was that many who pretended to be disgusted by me during the day would discreetly knock on my door at night. Where they went wrong was that they expected an eager, compliant me. I sent every one of them packing. I was fine with not drinking tea for the rest of my life rather than submit to those lecherous people.

It was actor Muktha who gave me a foothold in the Malayalam industry. We share a wonderful chemistry, and it was she who made me a familiar name in the South Indian movie industry. As time passed, my contacts grew, and I gained healthy and meaningful friendships in the Malayalam cinema industry. My friends included Mamta Mohandas and Rimi Tomy, who never let go of an opportunity to promote me. I began to get work. Actresses and their mothers or immediate families began to prefer me as I am a non-threatening presence. There have been several instances of makeup artists misbehaving with actresses or spreading salacious stories about them. A makeup artist of yore went on record in a magazine about how he would give oil massages to famous actresses. I am like a human shield. Not only are they safe with me, I also tactfully prevent any potential wardrobe malfunction. I was quite in demand.

The heartburn this created among my colleagues was what probably led to the arrival, on one of my sets, of the president of the Make-up Artists Association, an organisation that mandates that only members be allowed to work in the movie industry. It helps regulate wages and personnel management and serves as a forum to raise grievances. It was the union of makeup artists. The president demanded that I be thrown out immediately as I was not a member of the association. As per the agreement between the different associations, a non-member cannot be allowed to work on the sets. I pleaded with the president and the film crew requested a special dispensation. Muktha, for whom I was doing the makeup that day, too came and asked the man to reconsider. He was adamant. I had to leave. The ban was only until I applied and was granted membership. But the public humiliation was unbearable. All this could have been settled with a phone call. It made me aware of the arrogance that people develop once they are in a position of power, however insignificant it may be. To be the president of a group of makeup artists means nothing in the world outside of the film industry. Yet the way he was carrying on made me wonder what he imagined he was in charge of. Tears filling my eyes, I told Muktha, 'I will be back once the membership is granted. A day will come when my work shines through and there will be no trace of this man.'

Call it what you will, but that is exactly what happened. He couldn't continue as a makeup artist and so opened an outlet for makeup products. The best part was that he invited me to inaugurate it! I acquiesced. The shop was a good one and he showed me around. I came to a stop in front of a machine and said, 'Oh good, you are selling this here.' To my complete amusement, he looked sheepish and said, 'I actually don't know what it does. Would you please explain?' That day I did the noblest thing I could imagine—I imparted knowledge to my enemy. I do not know what became of him or his shop as I use a completely different range of makeup products.

It is ironic that in my village, and in the houses and public places where I worked, I was never subjected to bullying—except from my brother. I was always treated with kindness. Yet it was in the film industry that celebrates art and polyphony that I had the bitterest of experiences. It deepened my belief that mere formal education is not enough to help mould an individual. People need to be made aware of the importance of acceptance and co-existence. It is important to embrace who you are rather than strive to keep up a public facade. Repressed people are fundamentally unhappy, and they seek relief in making others miserable. Let's all live and laugh openly, and the world will automatically become a happy place. Having found security among my friends and well-wishers, I felt like it was time to be born again.

Chapter Two

A person's story ideally begins at the time of their birth. Sometimes, if they have a sense of grandeur or legacy, it might begin with the lives and times of their forefathers. Anyway, it is said that we cannot choose to be born, let alone decide when we want to be born. I often think that that is how people are born ahead of their time; sometimes when I read about ultra-conservative or regressive people, I realise they were born much after their time. I am one of the lucky few who got to choose the time, date and even place of their birth. This new, self-determined life that I am leading now is nothing short of a miraculous birth. How else can one explain an unremarkable, rather quiet boy from a back-of-the-beyond village in Kollam, Kerala, undergoing the transformation that I did?

Those around me think I am enigmatic, that it is difficult to read my mind. To them I smile and say, 'My mind runs at a great speed to keep up with my thoughts. I have such dreams, such ambitions that sometimes it makes me breathless.' I am not an enigma. My thought process is simple. I hate deceit. It disgusts me to meet or associate with double-faced people. I am often asked to understand and sympathise with people who lead a 'normal' life by day and dress up in women's clothing at night. I am asked to allow people who are leading lives as fathers and husbands to come participate in competitions and festivals meant for transpeople. To all of them, I say a firm no. Being transgender is not a temporary state of being nor is it simply about cross-dressing. It is about the desire to transform into who you want to be known as and seen as. That feeling, that identity does not go away just because you changed your clothes. And if it is not terrible enough that you are lying to yourself when you lead this double existence, you are also cheating your spouse and children. How is that fair to them? What am I supposed to understand or sympathise about this?

Countless transpeople have lost their lives in the struggle to help our community lead a life of dignity. Countless members of our community have undergone exploitation, assault, heartbreak, depression, just because they did not hide who they were. Hardly anyone in this country has been convicted of crimes against transpeople. I remember watching a documentary called *Call Her Ganda* (2018) about a Filipino transperson who was killed by an American soldier in a hotel room. The Philippines is a military base for the USA. The incident sparked outrage in the Philippines as the law dictates that American soldiers cannot be prosecuted in Filipino courts. The trans community came out in full force to get justice for Ganda (she took that name because it means 'beautiful'), and the court sentenced the soldier to be imprisoned. But the American government ensured that the sentence was never carried out. The documentary brought mixed feelings to the surface for me. I was inspired by the way the community stood together to fight for their sister. It was also moving to see the public supporting her cause. Ganda's was a landmark case in the Philippines. But the way power and money won in the end saddened me. I knew the situation was not very different in India, where cases of crimes against transpersons go unreported or unsolved.

Given the state of affairs, I cannot condone people remaining ensconced in the comfort of their homes, leading multiple lives. We have to accept that being transgender is not just about identity, it is also about activism. Every trans body is a site for a revolution. It is a way of telling society, 'Look! Here I am! Here I always will be. There are more like me ... we are just like you ... we made a choice, and we are brave. So, move on ... let us live our lives!' I wished someone would make a change that would help people lead their lives without fear and shame so that families would open their hearts instead of shutting their doors. And I asked myself, 'Who are you waiting for?' I decided not to wait for someone else to do it. I did it.

I wanted an organisation dedicated to working for transpeople, but one that went beyond just creating awareness about AIDS and safe sex practices. I wanted to build a welfare organisation that worked to create opportunities, to provide access to education and livelihood. I wanted universal rights for my people. And if I wanted all this, I had to work. That is when the idea of Dhwayah began to take root in my heart. With the unconditional support of my friends Sheethal Shyam and Soorya, I decided to take the plunge and thus, with seven members, the Dhwayah Transgender Arts and Charitable Society was established.

The charter rules state that Dhwayah will work towards creating avenues for transpeople to live and work with dignity. It is not fair to sit around on our hands waiting for government aid. What we ought to do is work, create an atmosphere where we have goodwill and visibility on our side to help the state create provisions for the community. I firmly believe in self-help being the best sort of help. Dhwayah's vision caused a lot of heartburn among other organisations working in this area. They had been going along by keeping transpeople in an abject state and had done nothing to pull them out of the mire of sex work. The situation had become so bad that most of the time, people automatically associated a transperson with sex work. And the lack of opportunities had turned so many of our community to sex work that they too began seeing it as a career choice—in some cases, the only career. Sadly, sex work pays a lot more than a regular but mostly menial job that members of our community might get due to their lack of education. The general suspicion that people view us with did not help either. These matters were of deep concern to us, and we decided on a definite step-by-step process. We agreed that education must be of primary importance as there are a lot of people among us who left home early due to persecution and could not complete their studies. So, what we needed was a continuing education programme and counselling services for young transpeople to help them stay home and finish their studies.

The 2014 NALSA verdict of the Honourable Supreme Court of India worked in our favour as the court too stressed on the need to implement policy reforms to help the community. Armed with this knowledge that we could not be ignored, we worked to ensure educational facilities for our people in the state. It was during a programme held in the auditorium of St Teresa's College, Ernakulam that the breakthrough came. In front of a capacity crowd of 3500 cheering girls, I asked the authorities if they would arrange for our community members to study a course there. I was told on stage that they would think about it. Having received a lot of official assurances from a number of offices in the past, I decided that this was not the time to be shy. So, I requested them to definitely look into the matter. I suppose it was our earnestness or the cheers of the girls, or both, that the college decided to conduct free English for Communication classes on weekends. It was an emotional sight for me to see my people attending the certificate course in uniforms and obediently taking down notes. I was also a student, though not a very regular one.

At the end of the course, we were given certificates. More than that, what made us happy was our sense of achievement. We could prove to ourselves and to others that there is more to us, that if we put our minds to something, we were unstoppable. The world around us was also opening up. The wave of progressive thoughts was finding its way into the country too. Questions were being raised in all parts of India about the condition of transpeople. The connectivity that we now had due to mobile phones and social media made us more aware of the movements in other parts of the country. We too celebrated when Manabi Bandyopadhyay became the first transperson to become the principal of a college. Each piece of news took us ten steps forward, be it Sathyasri Sharmila, the first transgender lawyer; Joyita Mondal, the first judge; Prithika Yashini, sub-inspector; or Shabnam Mausi, the first legislator. We felt a beautiful kinship with these individuals, though we did not know any of them personally. I wanted these achievements to be replicated in Kerala. We too dared to dream. Through extensive outreach and using the skills of our community members, Dhawayah built up an impressive array of outreach activities.

We decided to take our case to the young people of the state. Our success at St Teresa's had emboldened us, and we decided to go all out when we were approached to perform by All Saints' College, Thiruvananthapuram. And perform we did! We gave the students a grand show with music, dance and a fashion show. At the end of it, we were mobbed! It made us feel like celebrities. We then performed in a number of prominent colleges and were also invited to several functions. The money was good, but it was never enough. I began putting my own money into the organisation. The informal helping hand that I used to extend to all those who asked me, now became official. I did not mind.

My job as a celebrity makeup artist was my life and my love. Once, my WhatsApp status was, 'My job is my boyfriend.' Before Dhwayah, I did not have many concerns. It was just my life and I needed to think only about my own subsistence. But now, life was different. My profession became a means to feed my activism. It is extremely rewarding, to say the least. To see your money transform lives is a blessing and I am proud of what Dhwayah has become. The annual gala that we hold is called Queen of Dhwayah; it is a massive affair with a personality pageant and an award ceremony where we felicitate the people who have done significant work for the community. My friends and well-wishers from the movie industry regularly make appearances, and we have had the pleasure of hosting prominent actors such as Madhubala (of *Roja* fame), Mammootty, Jayasurya, Mamta Mohandas and many others. Now, the Queen of Dhwayah has become the meeting point for transpeople and activists from all over the state and has seen the genesis of a great many ideas.

In the middle of my hectic professional and social life, there is very little space for the concept of the personal. I have been a sensitive person since childhood. When I learned to recognise myself, I realised that my mind was like how a woman's mind is commonly perceived to be. While the boys went for a little rough and tumble on their way to school, I would stop to tease the touch-me-nots. I wanted to smell the flowers and walk daintily. My books were always neatly arranged and my handwriting was neat. I hated football and all the rough games that the boys played. I wanted to do chores around the house. If you are going to accuse me of having replicated the traditional, patriarchal stereotypes of women when I did household work, all I can say is that only such women were available for me to model myself on.

As I said before, I wanted to do something meaningful with my life. For that, I needed to be unfettered, to fly free like a bird, to come and go as I please. With a partner, this might not always be possible. I have seen, quite often, that the partner becomes fair game for other transpeople. They imagine that half the work—identifying a potential companion—is done, so it is very convenient to make a play for him. It has pained me to see people walk in with one transperson and eye another. I have seen messages being sent and those messages being deleted immediately on reading, and clandestine meetings in hotel rooms leading to tearful and noisy confrontations. Many people enter into open relationships, just to retain their partners who insist on polyamory. Community ties weaken. Hostility builds up. I don't like all this drama and filth being dragged through my life. A friend once looked at the lines on my palms and remarked that they were very clear and straight. She pointed out that this indicates that I lead a trouble-free life. The truth is that I prefer keeping things uncomplicated. Above all, I want to keep my dignity intact. This is why there is no place in my life for even a casual fling.

I get a lot of proposals on Facebook, declarations of undying love, people accusing me of deliberately ignoring their entreaties. All I have to say by way of explanation is: let us just try to make the world around us a better place for those in need, those suffering, those considered less than human on account of their refusal to live a lie. It is also important that my personal life be as free of blemishes as my public life. Only ten per cent of transgender relationships stand the test of time. There is no accountability or stability. Partners play the Russian Roulette, picking and dropping their trans lovers at will. This has caused transpeople to be seen as promiscuous or scheming. I want to change that. I want to tell my dear ones that we don't need a relationship to feel secure. This feeling of community that we have is enough. It will sustain us.

On some evenings, just as dusk sets in, I sit down with a cup of tea and think about the turn that my life has taken. While working in the brick kiln or going door to door selling books, I never dreamt that there would come a time when I would travel to exotic locations and sample so many cuisines. I have visited Switzerland, Germany, the UAE, Malaysia, Thailand and Australia as well as almost all the scenic locations in India. In most of these countries, what I enjoyed the most was the sense of freedom. There were no nudges, no prying eyes, no disparaging comments. There was nothing exotic about me. I was just another person out on the town, having a good time. I did want someone with me to enjoy the snow, the sand or the colours of these places but, like I said, sense prevails over the desires of momentary pleasures. I am also wary of being disrespected by my partner, if I have one. Being in the industry, I have heard the way people talk of the people they have slept with. There is derision in their tone, a dismissal. I don't want to take a chance like that. This is why I make sure I keep a distance from nefarious elements whom I come across in the course of my work. Associating with these disruptive elements can help me lead a glitzy life but there is a very high price to pay. Often, I read of people of minor fame being arrested from drug parties and raves, and I realise that I know them. This means if I so chose, I could have been at the party, getting stoned. If I had merely attended the party and had been taken into custody, irrespective of whether I was under the influence of narcotics or not, it would have become news. All the goodwill, the standing that I had built up would have vanished in an instant. I know better than to give in to temptation because I have come up the hard way. My success is built on hard work, tears and single-minded dedication. And I have linked my life's goals to my career. I am not willing to throw those away for anything or anybody.

I have no regrets. My children are always around me. Nothing can diminish the pride and happiness that I feel when I hear them call me 'Amma'. And I believe I have always done the right thing by them. I have been fortunate enough to see two of them get married and lead lives of great happiness. On their respective wedding days, I was ecstatic. I dressed the brides in all their finery as their mother and gave them my blessings. Not only did I know the joy of giving my daughters away, I also had the pleasure of welcoming a daughter into the family. My son Vihaan Peethambar got married to Rajasree. It was a wedding to remember. We all had so much fun. All these weddings and the good times we had at them made me wish that life could always be like this—lives being led with happiness, understanding and simplicity. There is so much love in the world if only we open our hearts. Why shut our windows and doors when it is bright and beautiful outside? It has become important for me to bring together families who have rejected their children, to bring reconciliation and healing to those hearts.

I often receive phone calls from young transpersons, asking me for advise and seeking guidance. Most want to run away from home as they are being harassed. A preliminary study by the Transgender Justice Board found that harassment is one of the main reasons that transpeople do not complete their education. This renders them vulnerable and unfit to gaining meaningful employment. Luckily for us, the younger generation is not like that. They listen to reason and are willing to wait it out before they take the plunge.

Of course, there are young people who find it impossible to live under the same roof as their families anymore and escape. Such children are often lost forever. The harrowing darkness of metro cities and their alleyways swallow them up. By the time they return, they are no longer children.

The trauma they suffered screams out of their eyes and it is only a lot of love and the community closing ranks around them that can erase it. I request parents to be patient with gender-dysphoric children and not make them hate themselves. The price these children pay because of your rejection is very high.

There is a young kid from Thrissur who calls me every now and then. Her parents thought they had produced a boy, but she soon began proving them wrong, and they began to resort to pressure tactics to make her give up. She reached out to me and I responded. She spends hours talking and messaging me about her plans and aspirations. I am happy that her spirit is not crushed. There are times when she says, 'Amma, I want to come be with you and live with you.' But I keep telling her to complete her school education. One day she called me in tears saying that school has become unbearable and that even the authorities were joining in in giving her a terrible time. This riled me up. I called up the principal and asked him if he was aware of the laws of the land and that it is an offence to torture a transgender kid. I told him very firmly, 'Don't make me come there. And as you know, jail is a terrible place.' The harassment has stopped.

At Vihaan's reception I met a young transman. He was being homeschooled by his mother and hoped to get admission into a hotel management course. I was very happy to meet his mother. I wished there were more parents like her who are sensitive to their children's minds and try to make their lives easier instead of imposing their own dreams and aspirations on the poor children.

This vicious cycle of families turning hostile, children running away from home, roaming the streets and becoming sex workers and drug mules, contracting addictions and disease and losing out on careers and opportunities, losing self-esteem and finally becoming dependent on handouts, must stop. Both Dhwayah and I are committed to this. The Transgender Justice Board has become a vocal presence in Kerala. Most of the members are either from Dhwayah or are associated with it. This helps us get a sympathetic hearing when we voice the grievances of the community or try to introduce schemes to benefit transpeople. It was a longstanding dream of Dhwayah that a youth festival be held for transpeople. This came true in 2019, when a grand festival showcasing the talents of transpeople was held in Thiruvananthapuram. The competitions were open only for transpeople registered with the Justice Board, to stop people from siphoning off the benefits from the festival. There was a huge number of participants from all the districts of Kerala and plenty of entries for the solo and group performances. I was heartened by the dedication of the participants who made time to come together for rehearsals or sent in videos of their dance steps through WhatsApp. One thing was clear—they were in it to win it!

This was not all. In the same year, we also held a sports meet for transpeople. Inaugurated by the Honourable Minister for Health, Social Justice, Women and Child Development, K. K. Shailaja Teacher, the sports meet drew participants and crowds alike. The spirit of sportsmanship was alive and well in all the competitions and it made me dare to dream of a transperson from this community participating in the Olympics one day. I am aware of the challenges faced by people like Caster Semenya and Duttee Chand, but times are indeed changing and dreams are what become reality. If someone had said a decade ago that they dreamt of a Transgender Justice Board, a youth festival or a sports meet for transpeople or that a transwoman from India would be the managing director of a multinational company, people would have laughed at them. And yet, here we are. I tell my children too: dream on—who knows which dream of yours will catch on and grow into a sturdy oak!

These achievements are not mine or Dhwayah's alone. We are just the carriers of the community's messages. By standing united and working single-mindedly to bring hope and help to our people, we will find them avenues for education and legal restitution. Kerala has now become one of the few states to introduce a quota for transpeople to study in colleges. There was an *adalat* (special hearing) to address the concerns of transgender youth. Thus, we are being heard; we are being seen. But that is not the final stop. There is so much to do and so little time.

Chapter Three

I sometimes think of my house in Kollam, where we were all born and grew up. That structure has since been demolished and I have a constructed a new house for my family to live in. It is large with a good number of rooms and a sweeping circular stairway. I wanted a house with many rooms for I would then be able to provide my community with a safe place to stay when they travel. Even when I am out of station, they stop by, check in on my mother, stay for a few days and leave. My family also comes together for celebrations there. It is a pleasant place to live in. But when I think of home, it is still that old, dilapidated house that bore the stamp of my ancestors. The front wall of the house had sustained water damage in the floods, but we never got around to repairing it. We just went about our lives incorporating the crumbling wall into our scheme of things. There was a tulsi plant in front of the house as a symbol of good luck and prosperity. There was also a sunflower plant which I loved. While sweeping the yard I used to look at the sunflower following the sun with its unwavering gaze. 'Such love, such ardent love the sunflower has for the sun,' I would think. I wondered if I would ever be someone's sun or sunflower—the very thought would set me blushing.

The land around our house was fertile and soft. It was alluvial and rich in nutrients owing to the river flowing nearby. On warm nights, we would spread our pallets and go to sleep in the front yard itself. Those were beautiful nights. There wasn't much—if any—pollution, so we could see the stars clearly in the black-violet sky. My brothers and sister would be talking, my parents would be recounting old stories and I would be in the midst of it all, the little one, listening and sometimes dozing off in the warm drone of voices. I used to think it was a blessing to be loved by one's family.

My mother had blue eyes and was very beautiful. My father was not very good-looking and had ordinary brown eyes which we all inherited. Father was not very strict and thankfully he never drank. But he smoked beedis. He was like a chimney and I would always associate beedis with my father. Mother was strict about hygiene and cleanliness. She was particular about traditional beliefs as well. In our part of the world, the mortar and pestle, or the *ammikallu*, on which we ground masalas or created the mix for the curries, is seen as akin to a mother. If my sister ground the spices and coconut and then simply rinsed the *ammikallu* with water without giving it a thorough cleaning, she would get a whack. My sister and I were the only ones who followed my mother's instructions to the letter. I supposed this was because we were both girls. My mother had the job of sorting and peeling fried cashews for the final packing and the smell would cling to her clothes and skin when she returned home after work. We would go rushing to her, clamouring to get the goodies and snacks that she would have bought from the tea stall on the way home from the factory, and then I would wrap myself around her leg to get an extra snack; this was the smell that I adored. She smelt of Cuticura powder, sweat and cashews. That is still the fragrance of love for me.

When I look back, there were lots of things that defined our daily routine. My mother began her day early at the factory, which left her no time to pack a lunch. We kids used to drink the *pazhamkanji*—a porridge of rice fermented overnight in water with fish curry or tapioca left over from the previous night—and rush off to school. My sister would stay back to do the household work. We used to get breakfast in school those days. The school was from morning to noon for one set of classes and then noon to evening for another set. After the morning shift, I would run to my house which was barely a kilometre and a half away and get a lunchbox and run back to school, this while my classmates would be finally returning home after dawdling around the school compound. I would run into the school building, eyes averted and lunchbox hidden, and go to Ummayya, the school cook and a friend of my mother's. She would take the lunch box and fill it with *kanji* and curry. I would rush home to give it to my sister. This was because my father would not have yet finished his work and collected his daily wages. Once he was done, he would come home, buying whole chillies, coriander seeds, fish, tapioca, rice and so on, and hand it to my sister to cook. Those were not the days of powdered spices in plastic packets. Everything came whole and in paper parcels bound by thin twine. My sister would set about cooking everything.

Images courtesy of Renju Renjimar

Renju Renjimar (left and centre) and her mother (right)

I learnt some saving techniques from my mother. She would never cook the entire stock of goods that my father bought. Every day, she would set aside a fistful or two of rice, some chillies and spices, and take a piece of tapioca, dry it and store it. Thus, in the monsoon, when my father found it difficult to find work, we had these rations to fall back on. And this was a woman who had never attended a school or a college or done a course in home economics or, as they called it in my day, home science—it was plain old common sense. These economies of household are what made Indian families what they are. These little holdings-back helped buy utensils, sewing machines and other items of daily necessities that would not otherwise be 'sanctioned' or would be pooh-poohed as unnecessary. These purchases or savings would then come into good use for the family itself. But often, the good sense and discipline of the lady of the house goes unappreciated. However, there is a value system slowly taking shape that celebrates economy in life, along with the values of conserving and protecting nature. Today, posh hotels are serving *pazhamkanji*. *Kanji* and its probiotic qualities are extolled. More and more people are trying their best to avoid use of plastic, and architects are incorporating the natural light and airflow of a place into their designs.

Gradually, as my brothers grew up and began contributing to household expenses, our situation improved. While we were not exactly starving before, we could now eat better, and the cow at home was also well cared for and, in turn, yielded more. We were better off, though not living in opulence. We were happy. There was a sense of well-being.

Finally, after many years, we got a loan from the Panchayat and we constructed a new house. But even today, in my mind, home means that old, run-down structure that housed so many of us in such safety and intimacy. Today, these concrete walls, air conditioners and everything luxurious cannot fill that void. I sometimes think that one day I will build myself a thatched-roof home, a small cottage, and live there. The floor would be polished with cow dung, thus keeping out heat and insects, and the walls would be smeared with lime. I was the one who used to smear cow dung on the floor at home, mixing it with soft mud and spreading it carefully and thoroughly. I have heard that, as time goes by, our wants also shrink. When that time comes, this is what I will do—go back to that life. When I think back, those were the happiest times of my life. Love was unconditional, food was scarce but there was a willingness to share, there was aspiration but no greed, and I felt protected. I had yet to experience the harrowing violence that continues to haunt me even today, particularly because it came from my most essential place of security—my family, my brothers. So, I was happy; if only everything had stayed the same. But then, like a river, life too flows and takes swift turns.

Just as I had fallen in love a couple of times, someone fell in love with me. This was during a train journey to Bangalore. I was sitting opposite a girl who was headed to Bangalore to train as a nurse. I was on a work-related journey. I had painted nails and kohl-rimmed eyes though I was in male attire. We got talking and exchanged addresses. Soon, she began writing to me. I would rarely respond. When I did reply, they would be polite replies. Then came a letter telling me that she was in love with me. She also sent along a brand-new Motorola mobile phone for us to talk with each other. I burst out laughing! I could not have been more apparent in terms of my identity in front of her and yet she had chosen to ignore the signs. In any case, it was very clear that I was not a 'man' in the conventional sense of things. Perhaps she mistook the comfort that one woman feels with another to be a romantic relationship between members of the opposite sex. It is interesting how people perceive us while we strive hard to be seen in a certain way. I suppose it is all in the gaze. The proposal, I rejected. The mobile phone, I kept.

Being in the makeup industry, I am quite aware of the way looks impact perception and how people read volumes into images. When I apply makeup on a person, in my mind, I am applying it on myself. It is I who am being made more beautiful. With that transposition, I strive to give my very best. The eyes are the most vocal part of a person's body. You can see the entire soul of the person when you look into their eyes. When I bend down to the person's eye level, I search within them for the story they wish to tell. I look for the person they are trying to be and bring that persona forward. This is why I try and speak a little with the person before we try on the final look.

I have built a companionable relationship with top actors such as Mamta Mohandas, Bhavana, Jyothirmayi, Priyamani and Remya Nambisan. These are but a few names that I am mentioning here. These women are family and there is nothing I would not do for them—and they for me. Bhavana is like my daughter and often the other actors would tease me if I tried to leave the set early. 'Your daughter is in town, isn't that why you are in such a hurry?' they would laugh. Thus began my career as a makeup artist for celebrities.

Some moments in this high-vaulting field come with their own rewards. As my work and techniques began to get noticed, I was asked to do makeup for none other than the *Roja* girl herself—Madhoo! Not only is she a huge name in Hindi cinema, she is one of the truly pan-Indian actors like Hema Malini, Jaya Prada, Sridevi, Khushboo and Nagma. Despite having stepped back from acting for a long while, she was still a name to reckon with in the industry. On the appointed day, Madhoo turned up. I was all agog with excitement. It was a defining moment for me. There was one small matter, though. Madhoo was steadfast in her refusal in allowing anyone but her own makeup artist to do her makeup. She also insisted on using the products that she had brought along. The organisers were in a fix. Very respectfully, Madhoo explained the situation to them and asked that her stipulations be met. There was no hostility or tantrum. So, feeling emboldened, I requested that I be given a small chance, and if found unsatisfactory, I would be more than happy to step aside. Perhaps out of the goodness of her heart or thinking that she had the option of rejecting me, she allowed me to proceed. Heart in mouth, I began. Madhoo was looking keenly into the mirror. I kept going. She hadn't yet objected. I felt a little bolder. I kept going. I had just done the outlines and was reaching for the fillers when she stopped me. 'Please stop,' she said. That was the end of the road, or so I thought. I stopped and withdrew my hands. She went up to her makeup person and spoke a few words and returned. She looked at me smiled and said, 'You please continue.'

I was overjoyed. It was a really happy moment for me to be acknowledged by someone like Madhoo. To be *chosen* by her. She made me her makeup person for yet another event and graced the stage of Dhwayah as a chief guest. It is a friendship I have always cherished.

In 2006 or 2007, I was at the Wills India Fashion Week in Delhi as part of Ambika Pillai's entourage. The who's who of Bollywood was either preparing to walk the ramp or was among the audience. I noticed a young model who was very sociable and chirpy. I did her makeup and she was very gracious in her reaction. It is always a matter of happiness to receive a word of praise from the subject of your attention. No matter how many people you help adorn, that one word of thanks or appreciation always strikes you with the happiness of the very first time. So, I made a mental note of her as I felt she would go really far. Later on, she appeared on film posters with Shah Rukh Khan himself, and a star was born. Deepika Padukone—I was finally able to put a name and legacy to the face! Years passed. On the sets of *Happy New Year*, while chatting with some technicians and crew from Kerala, my name came up and she told them that she remembered me! Much later, at the Asia Vision Awards where she was a guest, I was waiting in the wings while she was called on and, in passing, she smiled and waved in recognition. I don't know if it's a signature move, but for me, it was a fangirl moment and I was happy that she remembered.

Slowly and steadily, I was beginning to get work at weddings as well. Malayalis had begun to spend a little more on weddings. Gone were the days when the biggest expenditure at weddings would be for video-recording. The aggressive advertisements for wedding sarees, bridal-attire collections and accessories had made the Malayali society look up to these as aspirational. The celebrations of weddings in films of the time had also given people ideas. The wedding of the daughter of the Indian tycoon Lakshmi Nivas Mittal, which had gone on in France for many days, awed Indian society. Prior to that, the grandeur of the wedding preparations of the adopted son of the late Tamil Nadu chief minister J. Jayalalithaa had sent us into paroxysms of disbelief. All this changed the sensibilities of wedding celebrations in India and, in particular, Kerala. The bride was not the only focus of the wedding, the immediate family was also making a splash. This made makeup a very important component of the wedding.

Noticing my work in films, I was invited for a trial for the bridal makeup of Ravi Pillai and Lekha Pillai's daughter Arathy Pillai. I was thrilled. Pillai is one of the biggest businessmen in the country, and the wedding was set to surpass anything we had seen in recent times. There was a mythological touch to the ambience and such beautiful flowers everywhere. And here I was, about to apply makeup to a young, hopeful woman embarking on a wonderful journey. That is all I thought about while I applied the brush to her face. I thought of her innocence, her fierce intelligence, the choices she had made, the values she held dear and the expectations she had from her life ahead. I put away all thoughts of tycoons, money, remuneration, the grand set design and so on. The result was such that they hired me on the spot and asked that I attend only to the bride and just the immediate family. This was a rare honour! And I made the most of it. I was also invited to the Arackal Palace for bridal makeup. My name appeared in the papers as the person who had done the makeup for these high-profile weddings. I began to get recognised. More offers began to pour in. My diary was filling up and I began to traverse the length and breadth of Kerala. People began to take pride in saying that I would be doing the makeup for the bride at the wedding. This is how I became a 'celebrity' makeup artist!

I don't take my work or the commitment it entails lightly. This position where I am today, being recognised for my work, being heard, being written about, is all on account of the work I do and the dignity it brings with it. That is why even when I got news of the passing of one of my brothers, I looked around me. I had four artistes waiting for me to do their makeup. They were relying on me and on the impeccable service that I was known to provide. So, I went on with the work, finished it and then attended the funeral. I was mourning him from within all the time. But I kept my emotions in check and kept going. People like me cannot afford to stop or stand still. I have come too far, and to turn back is impossible.

I keep thinking that these high, posh places are where many of my community generally are not invited to. But because I have a trade, I have training and knowledge, these doors are open to me. My belief in education and gaining a skill was thus reinforced. I have considered myself quite lucky that most of the people I met were of a positive mindset and did not look to exploit or mislead me. I used to be a rather gullible person who would easily trust others. A lot of bitter experiences changed my outlook and sobered me. But my gang of girls—my actor friends and my daughters and sisters from the community—always ensure that I do not get lost in a mist of seriousness. There are times when I do go crazy and end up playing the fool or goofing around. I suppose it is my own way of blowing off steam or reclaiming my old, innocent self.

One of the first things I did when I began to earn good money was to buy a car. Earlier, I had to use public transport and would often be teased mercilessly. People can be quite insensitive. They would prod me or pass rude comments questioning my gender or my sexuality. Sometimes I would be picked on by the police for no reason other than that they were possibly feeling bored and wanted to have fun. There were times when I was beaten black and blue by policemen and my family had to come get me. The spectre of Section 377 loomed over people like me even when we were trying to earn an honest living. Introduced during the time of the British, Section 377 was meant to criminalise sexual activities 'against the order of nature'. I find that sentence unnatural. But it gave law enforcement extensive powers. It was on the strength of that section that they brutalised me. It is not that those policemen were unknown to me. They knew me quite well, were familiar with my work and my character, and yet they would resort to this sort of casual violence. My powerlessness would have been their source of enjoyment.

Once I was walking through my hometown in Kollam and I was picked up by the police. At the police station, a cane was threaded through my fingers, pressing hard, causing pain to shoot through my nerves. I was beaten on my soles, on my back and on every square inch of my body. I still wonder why that happened to me. These are the sorts of instances that often push transpersons towards substance abuse and depression. There are far serious crimes and glaring inequalities in society that can be solved through active legal intervention, and yet it is on the bodies of innocent transpersons and similar underprivileged individuals that power is exerted. This sort of injustice has been the tipping point for many members of my community. I have witnessed it firsthand. This is why, through Dhwayah, we seek to intervene legally and try to prevent such atrocities from ruining the mental and physical well-being of our people.

So, to prevent further harassment and prejudice, I bought a car. A white one. I felt empowered. It was a matter of great pride for me. And now I own a fleet of cars—a Thar, a Jeep, an Innova, an i10, and a BMW sedan. I have a great collection of watches as well. I have learnt that, in this world, it is important to keep up appearances. I have observed that you are as good as the things you wear or the vehicle you own. These things open swanky doors for you and create access. That is what is called keeping up pretences.

Buying a car, dressing well, wearing expensive watches and using branded things is how I apply makeup on myself every day. They are accoutrements I use to keep exploitation, prejudice, disrespect and disdain at bay. These are but instruments that I use to combat power and its blatant, unapologetic exercise. There is another attire that I wear within, which I alone can see when I look in the mirror. I am dressed like my mother, smelling of cashew and smoke, hands callused from hard labour, body stringy from work and exertion. Inside, deep in the recesses of my heart, there is a home with a damaged wall, a tulsi and a sunflower plant where a family sleeps under the stars.

Chapter Four

In the *Mahabharata* there are three sisters, Amba, Ambika and Ambalika, the princesses of Kashi. Bheeshma, the regent and chief advisor of the kingdom of Hastinapur, abducts them from their *swayamvara* ceremony for his stepbrother, King Vichitraveerya. Thus, the princesses are robbed of their chance to choose their own husbands. One among them, Amba, goes up to Bheeshma after they reach Hastinapur and tells him that she has already made up her mind to marry Shalva, the king of Saubha. Her father and the prospective groom are all in favour of the match but this abduction has created an obstacle. Bheeshma asks Amba to go to the groom of her choice and proceeds to arrange for the wedding of the other two princesses to Vichitraveerya.

Upon going to Shalva, Amba is met with a crushing rejection. She is told in no uncertain terms that he cannot accept someone taken away as spoils in an act of aggression. He feels that marrying Amba would be a stain on his manhood. Amba goes back to Bheeshma and asks that he marry her as she is reduced to this condition due to his actions. Bheeshma refuses to marry her as he is steadfast in his vow of celibacy. An enraged Amba commits herself to severe penance. Such is the fury of her penance that Lord Shiva comes before her and grants her any boon she desires. She asks that she gets to cause Bheeshma's death.

It was said that only Bheeshma could choose the time of his death. In order to hasten Bheeshma's death, Amba chooses to die in a fire and be reborn as Shikhandini, the daughter of King Drupada. As Drupada wants a son, he is granted a boon that his daughter will later become a son. So, Drupada raises this daughter as a son and gets her married to a princess. The bride complains to her father that her husband is actually a woman. The king sends his men to investigate, and Shikhandini panics and flees into the forest, where she encounters a *yaksha* who agrees to temporarily exchange sexes with her. The people who came to check finds Shikhandini to be a male. He is called Shikhandi. Thus, in the *Mahabharata*, Shikhandi serves as a human shield for Arjuna (also his brother-in-law) who then shoots arrow after arrow at Bheeshma to fell him. Bheeshma recognises Shikhandi as Shikhandini, Amba reborn, and refuses to fight, perceiving her as a woman. Later, Shikhandi is tamely killed by Ashwatthama.

I have often thought about this story—of bodies and what they mean. The body is such a corporeal, physical presence that it could be perceived as the greatest truth. It houses mechanics of such simplicity and yet such complexity. The simplest act of moving a finger is the result of so many processes, all of which happen possibly faster than the speed of light. In an instant, sometimes, we can recall an entire lifetime and yet it takes a literal lifetime to live out these customs, practices, rituals and laws. There is an interior life that the body leads, which incorporates the biological processes and the psychological process. Then there are the exterior processes, those of appearance, presentation and positioning. There is truth in the interior workings. The external trappings often lie. We paint ourselves different from who we might actually be. We colour our hair to look younger, wear loose or fitting clothes to appear bulkier or thinner than we are, grander or poorer than we are, taller than we are—the list of deceptions is endless.

But what if, one day, we match our exterior to our interior and present ourselves exactly as we feel? Did Amba have to die so Shikhandi could be born? Was it a literal death or a symbolic one? Was it an act of crossing over that was construed as death? Because when you think about it, such crossings are rebirths. *Nirvaan*, meaning 'born again', that's what we call them, those who survive their gender-affirmation surgeries, and we offer thanks to the goddess.

From the time I could remember, I was unhappy with my body. I did not understand it. It was different from what I wanted it to be. In my mind, my body had to resemble that of my mother or sister. Yet here it was, with a hardness in the limbs and a tendency to become muscular. The boys would play rough games of football and try and force me to join them. I would stay away as much as I could. They would all jump into the pond in shorts or short towels. I was horrified at having to display myself thus. The boys and girls found me strange. But I was comfortable in the invisible veil that I was wearing. To keep up appearances, I would style my hair in the manner of Mammootty, the reigning star of the day. I wore pants, but opted for longish shirts or half-kurtas. I would shrink from the over-friendly affections of my male friends. My other friends who were like me would meet up and we would have a grand time discussing boys and what not.

When I began to come into my own as a makeup artist, I decided that it was time to let my identity become apparent, at least by degrees. So, I continued to paint my nails, grew out my hair, slowly changed my clothing style and also began to wear more makeup. Initially I was met with curious glances, but soon, in the bustle of life and the rush of work, these glances lost their edge. When I became more vocal about my transformation, I was often asked, what did I mean by becoming a woman? What did I think was the meaning of being a woman?

My answer rarely satisfied people, but for me, it was to own the body that matched the voice of the woman inside me. To love a man with all the softness, coyness and tempestuousness of a woman. To keep things in order, to exult in my fragility and my strength. Perhaps these are stereotypes; perhaps 'real' women are much more than all this; and I respect the journeys of biological females. I only say that my journey is also unique and comes with its own challenges. To give up a seat at the table of 'power', especially in a patriarchal society like ours, requires real courage and total conviction. And I have that. I have never wavered in the truth about my identity. It is only recently that I set about making the dream come true.

It was a cherished moment for me when I got my passport. If a car represented freedom of movement for me, a passport represented the entire world opening up for me. But initially I used to be stopped at immigration as the passport said 'Male' and I was not very male-looking. I was subject to scrutiny and occasional insults. This was also one of the reasons why I decided it was time to effect a transformation. There were many countries where I was very comfortable in my clothes and with who I was. There were no restrictions on movement or travel. But some countries were strict and it caused me a lot of embarrassment. Now my passport reflects who I am. In fact, every single identification document announces who I am—boldly. Why should my journey to my truth be any less than anyone else's?

**

The Goddess Gives Breasts and Vagina?

I walk in thoughts of being a girl
and sit and laugh. Family
and society heckle me.
At night, I fondle my

non-existent breasts.
Legs squeezed together, I create
my own intimate space.
When sleep drags my lids down,
I weep appeals to the Goddess.
I would wake in the morning with the hopes of
Goddess-given breasts and vagina.
Time rolled on,
family and friends heckled on.
Lying there on the surgery table,
I dreamt of breasts and vagina.
I opened my eyes and
looked around.
My chest felt heavy, a soreness between my legs.
Once again, I woke crying.
This time because my dream came true.
The Goddess gave me breasts and vagina.
Family and friends went on heckling.

Renju Renjimar

 Scan the QR code to listen to Sonya J. Nair recite this poem.

 Scan the QR code to listen to the Malayalam version in Renju Renjimar's voice.

The process of undergoing this transformation is no less arduous than Amba's penance. The subsequent surgeries are just as painful as her act of shedding her body to become Shikhandini. SRS or Sex Reassignment Surgery, or gender affirmation surgery, as we call it these days, is not something one can have at a moment's notice. One has to be mentally, physiologically and physically prepared. First should come a sense of conviction about the entire process and the demands it can make on one's time, the toll it can take on the health, and the readiness to submit to medical advice. Then there are a series of injections one has to take to prepare the body to accept the incoming onslaught. I had a series of surgeries performed in preparation and these I got done in the best places I could afford, after multiple consultations and informed opinions. I sculpted every part of my body with care because there would be no going back after this, and the physical and mental scarring of surgeries going wrong is horrendous.

There was the case of Ananyah, my dear friend who ended up killing herself as she couldn't bear the pain of her surgeries. The bleeding would not stop and on some days, she was too weak even to be able to change the pads. She had ardently desired the surgery, but had not mentally prepared to face the complications and intricacies it entailed. Her dependence on painkillers grew and she became depressed; there was also the fact that others seemed to be moving on while she was stuck in the never-ending cycle of pain. It all just got too much for her and resulted in the loss of a vivacious, promising young person. She had such talent, such brilliance. She often took on the role of presenter for Dhwayah events. There are numerous such cases where lack of adequate mental, monetary or medical support resulted in botched surgeries and a lifetime of pain and crushed dreams.

It's not just transwomen who face this problem; it's also transmen. There should be a comprehensive policy and protocol that must be followed; and only after adequate clearance must these procedures be sanctioned. The Government of Kerala offers monetary assistance for gender affirmation surgeries and quite a lot of private medical service providers have also entered the fray. The best thing would be to find a team of doctors who are committed to quality rather than speed.

I thought of it as a journey, one step at a time. The hormone injections, the enhancements and finally the transformation. At each juncture, I felt a sense of elation. My body welcomed each change with open arms. It was like being embraced by warm water. I let the softening of my skin, the emergence of curves, the changing cadences of my voice wash over me. I revelled in the way my clothes fit. I made sure that my breast enhancements felt just right. It was not about the size, it was about the way I wanted to carry myself. I wanted my transformation to bring out the underlying sense of elegance that I aspired to. Looking back, I understand that I wanted my body to radiate my personality.

I underwent hormone therapy for quite a while so as to be at the optimum state for the surgeries. During the hormone treatments, I would closely watch myself for the changes that were expected to follow. I would celebrate each of these little milestones—when the body changes, softens, forms contours, when breasts begin to sprout, there is a newfound tenderness. When I went in for breast augmentation procedures, I looked at the various options available, the sizes, and imagined how they would feel on me. Finally, I chose a size that I was most comfortable with. Like decorating a new home that I would be moving into, I began to put together various parts of me. Slowly but surely, I was emerging.

The day had dawned, and it was time for the last leg of the surgery that would complete my transformation. This is one of the longest and riskiest surgeries there is. I was able to recollect the whole process in my head as the doctors had explained it very vividly. It was etched on my brain. The first stage is the excision of the penis. Then an external vagina is created. The skin of the penis is used to create a segment of the vaginal passage. It must be monitored well as it has a tendency to close as part of the healing process. Then a portion of the intestine is used to further create a vaginal passage. This part is quite tricky as it must be created between the anus and the bladder. This requires a delicate process of drilling between the two parts. If the bladder is damaged during the process, there will be perpetual incontinence and if the anus is damaged, it results in a lifetime of having to carry a colostomy bag.

Thinking of all this, I was going to go into surgery. My hair was braided into two plaits and I lay on the stretcher to be wheeled into the operating theatre for a surgery I had waited eighteen long years for. When I glanced up, I saw the blank ceiling, lights and nothing more. I wondered if this insipid sight was the last thing I would ever see. Seven surgeries would be performed simultaneously on me. I went under while not being sure of waking up.

After fourteen hours of surgery, the doctor woke me up. I was thoroughly groggy from the sedatives. I tried to lift my hands but they had been tied to the bed—my feet restrained as well. Apparently, this is done to minimise movement and protect the stitches. I wailed to the doctor, 'Doctor, something has happened to my hands. I want to do makeup, doctor. How will I do makeup without my hands?' The kind doctor assured me that everything would be alright. Soon I gained complete consciousness and then it was time to wait and watch. They made me walk to see if there was any problem in movement. Passing gas is considered one of the signs of a successful surgery. I managed this well before the expected time, and, remarkably, also passed stools after more than twenty-four hours without food. This meant that the surgery was a great success.

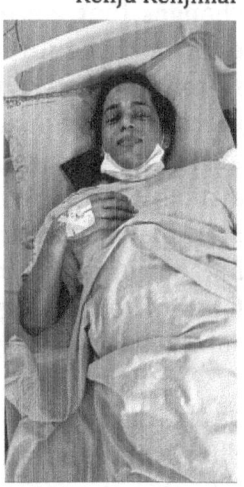

Image courtesy of Renju Renjimar

After the surgery

I was discharged after five days, which the doctors told me was not the norm. I walked to my car, got in and was driven home. I got out of the car and walked into my house, into the bedroom and lay down, without assistance. On the seventh day, I was supposed to go to the hospital to have the last of the tubes protruding out of me removed. On the morning of the seventh day, the tube simply came out on its own, sparing me a trip to the hospital. Post-op care is very important and there too, my friends and daughters rallied around me. Someone would be on constant video call with me and others would be hovering around, anticipating my every need. It is indeed a blessing to be so loved, so cared for.

While I was away at the hospital for the surgery, my daughters and the members of my community, who are dearer than blood to me, prayed for my safe return and they promised the goddess that I would have a *jalsa* ceremony if the surgery was successful. Normally I don't stand for rituals, but such was their ardent desire and excitement at getting a chance to celebrate a special day in my honour, that I had to give in. There is a general complaint that I don't host celebrations to mark my birthdays and similar festive occasions. I am just strange that way! Every year, the first batch of my students from the beauty academy host a small get-together on my birthday and no matter where I am, I make sure that I try and be there with them, these wonderful women whose journeys into financial independence and lives of dignity coincided with my journey as a teacher.

So, I agreed to the *jalsa*. Surya Ishaan, my daughter and student, set about arranging everything with my other daughters. Sheethal Shyam, the activist, Daya Gayathri, Sadiya and Harini Chandana were all there along with many members of the community. The house was decked with marigold flowers and tulsi. A large photo of Goddess Santoshi Mata was placed and fruit, flowers, incense sticks and oil lamps were brought in. The lamps were lit, the incense sticks gave off a wonderful fragrance, the flowers and fruit, symbols of prosperity and femininity, were offered to the goddess. Everyone sang *bhajans* in praise of the goddess. I was dressed in green, the colour of fertility and prosperity. My mother was standing next to me. I closed my eyes and prayed with folded hands.

'Everyone I love is here, with me O Goddess. Bless us and keep us safe. Give us the courage to tread uncharted territories. There is so much to do and so little time. What have you decided for me? What do I do? Where do I go from here?'

But before she could answer, my mother tapped my hand. I looked at her. In her smile and in her eyes, I found the antidote to all my apprehensions.

Here was my mother who once thought that she had given birth to one daughter and three sons, and then saw one of those boys completely change the narrative of that life, turn destiny on its head, swim against all tides and be reborn.

She said, 'I was your mother in your other birth. Now you are born again, the goddess is your mother. May she always protect you.'

This unlettered woman, from a scratch-in-the-ground sort of village, showed more sagacity and enlightenment than those many people who have travelled the world, speak two or three languages, are public figures and yet have not emerged from their Neanderthal self.

My mother tied the *lacha*, a string that has black beads and a *tali*, a pendant signifying a married woman, for me. I don't wear it often, but it is very special. We went to the beach at midnight and made the offering of a pot of milk. I returned home and took a bath. Only then was I allowed to look in a mirror, as it is forbidden to see one's reflection until the *jalsa* ceremony is complete.

Today, when I wrap a saree around me, it is with a sense of deep satisfaction. It makes me happy to see me as I am. And that makes me want to spread positivity. I believe that only those who are unhappy deep inside try to restrict the freedom of others or stifle others' spirits. There are times when I do not understand why anyone would have a problem with a human being trying to be happy by changing deeply personal identity markers that are exclusive to them. Aspects such as these do not affect anyone else. How can anyone be repelled by people wanting to become better versions of themselves? We encourage the weak to build up muscle strength, the vulnerable to learn self-defence, the underprivileged to gain an education. But when a person wants to change their gender, all hell breaks loose and everybody has an opinion—an unsolicited opinion. But I know change will come. It has already set out and will sweep over our shores like a mighty downpour.

Having the body of my choice is not the final frontier for me. I want to explore the possibilities of integrating it further with the desires that my mind has been nurturing. I want to carry a child to term and give birth, to experience the pain that women feel at the time of delivery. When my sister-in-law was admitted to hospital for her delivery, I went to visit her. Her room was adjacent to the labour room and I saw a fleeting glimpse of a woman screaming her heart out in the throes of delivery pain. That image stayed with me. I wondered how it would be to be her. I imagined her holding her little one and the thoughts that would be running through her mind. I want to experience that. I am often told that I am idealising this notion, that, in reality, the pain is so intense that it feels as if the nerves are being shredded and the pelvic floor is expanding. Some women have even suffered fractures. I know all this. But what if that, for me, is aspirational, if I consider it the ultimate validation of my identity? I want to hold my baby in my arms and feel that pain melting away in the tears of joy that I shed.

Thus my body that came from the very depths of my mother, that was cherished by my family when I was a baby and then a child, which was later abused, crushed mercilessly by those same people, was finally cast away. I travelled the world, chose the best, thought, re-thought and then made decisions. I fashioned a body of my choice. This is who I choose to be and this is who I wish to be seen as. The identity that I carried around in my heart has finally been mirrored in my body. After years and years, I felt free. I was free. And I revelled in the beauty of me. It does not matter who you see when you look at me. When I look at myself in the mirror, I see eyes shining with joy, I see a woman with poise and a sense of destiny. I see the proud swell of her chest and her smooth shoulders. I see her lustrous hair and her lips and cheeks. She is woman—whole woman, every inch of her. And I, who gave birth to her, I, who am my own mother, am happy. I laugh—and laugh—and the universe, indeed all of Creation, laughs with me.

Image courtesy of Renju Renjimar

Chapter Five

Yesterday, she wanted to deck herself up
But she had to wait for him to shed himself.
He, in the depths of the night,
lined his eyes with kohl—as her—
drew a bindi, applied lipstick—becoming more her—
like the moon that gains fullness with each passing night.
Someone knocked on the door.
She softened her voice and said, 'I have slept.'
She wished day would never break.
When the rooster crows,
He would be back, piece by piece,
distancing himself from her
through a name, a form, a family, society, an Aadhar Card,
a driver's licence.
He emerges from the ashes of her.
She waits in the shadows of the night.

—Renju Renjimar

 Scan the QR code to listen to Sonya J. Nair recite this poem.

There is, in the *Mahabharata*, the story of Chitrangada, the daughter of King Chitravahana of the kingdom of Manipur. During his period of penance for having barged into the private space of his brother Yuddhishthira and his wife Draupadi, Arjuna travels to Manipur and is captivated by

Chitrangada's beauty. He approaches the king for her hand in marriage. The king initially refuses as he has raised Chitrangada to be a *putrika*—one whose descendants will be king. Hence he does not like the idea of his only child going away with her husband and leaving the kingdom without an heir. Arjuna promises to stay with her till she bears a child and then leave her behind in Manipur. The king agrees to the wedding. Arjuna lives with Chitrangada for three years, has a son called Babruvahan by her and then embraces her and leaves. Years go by, and the Great War is fought. Finally, Yuddhishthira performs an Ashwamedha Yagna—a ritual in which a white horse is let loose and is accompanied by warriors. The lands through which the horse passes unchallenged pay tribute to the king and accept his suzerainty. If the horse is stopped, then battle breaks out between the two factions until a clear winner emerges. Kings do not undertake the Ashwamedha Yagna lightly; only one who is sure of his dominance even ventures to perform it. At one point, near Manipur, a young man stops the horse and is challenged by Arjuna. Showers of arrows flow from both sides and Arjuna is surprised at the young man's skill. He is struck by the arrows and falls unconscious. Hearing of this battle, Chitrangada comes running to try and prevent a potential tragedy. But she is too late. Arjuna seems to have succumbed to his injuries. At this moment, Uloopi, the Naga princess and yet another of Arjuna's wives, comes there with the Nagamani, a divine gemstone that can bring the dead back to life. She uses it and revives Arjuna. She explains that Arjuna was cursed by the Vasus to be killed by his own son as he had killed Bheeshma, who was actually the eighth Vasu who had to live out his life on earth due to the intervention of King Shantanu. That curse has now been lifted by this incident.

In his dance drama *Chitra*, the legendary poet Rabindranath Tagore had a slightly different take on

Chitrangada. He portrays her as a girl whose father brings her up as a boy, a prince, to rule the kingdom. She falls for Arjuna's charm, vigour and bravery, and finally has a son by him. This is the narrative that was the inspiration for Rituparno Ghosh's wonderful film *Chitrangada*. The film portrayed a person in the throes of love, trying to become someone they were not.

I loved Rituparno Ghosh—loved their personality, their films and that sense of fluidity that existed in the way they carried themselves. I have keenly observed the way their characters talked, the sense of logic these characters exuded when discussing relationships or genders or their lives. I have wished I were a character in a Rituparno film. It would be an honour, of course, to work alongside them in their films, especially since we have the same idea of aesthetics, or at least that is the impression I have from the films I have watched. But I really wanted to be a character in those stories—where people talk with a sense of history hanging over them, where they are definite about their desires and what they want out of life and go out to get it despite everything, despite life itself. I think that is the charm of cinema. It brings the stories of its characters to a definite conclusion. Well, most movies do that.

For me, this fascination with films transcends Ghosh's works. I love films and enjoy losing myself in them. I daydream of being the lead actor in one of those songs, dancing in sync with the music and lyrics. In fact, it is this love for performance that made me start my own Instagram account. I post snippets of performances of songs, segments of my life and trips abroad, and so on. I am quite active on Instagram and, until recently, had a huge following of 1,90,000. Sadly, the account was hacked. I was not deterred and opened a new account; the current number of my followers stands at 3,40,000 and counting.

Instagram and similar social-media platforms have brought people closer to the lives of celebrities and we often see their reactions to the comments of their fans going viral. I too reply to most comments. Most comments are on my singing or dancing. These days, I post songs about maternal love. I have an overwhelming desire to become a mother. It may be biologically impossible to bear a child. But that does not have to stop me from wanting a child. When I tie a bump to my stomach and drape myself in a saree and look in the mirror, I see a woman in the early delights of pregnancy. I see her stroking her stomach, whispering endearments to the little life within. When the saree is parted and the bump stands revealed for what it is—a rolled-up bundle—the hurt is immense. But I hide my pain and smile, sing and dance. Sometimes my goofy acts anger my followers who term them 'clownish' or 'buffoonery'. If I wear short clothes and dance, some people get offended and ask that I wear only sarees and present only my traditional self. To them I respectfully say, 'This is my space. I will be what I want to be here. You are welcome to watch. But please don't try and limit me within the images that you carry of me in your minds. I have come too far and fought too hard for my autonomy and will not give it up for love or money.'

That is what I fear—this boxing in. People who have professed their love for me and whom I have let come close to me soon start to try and take me for granted. They try and control aspects of my life as though I was chronically incapable of living my own life till then. I have been in love, and I did and possibly still do care very deeply. But those were all relationships that I nurtured in my heart; I never expressed anything—I don't know why. Perhaps it seemed inelegant. Or I did not want to spoil the serenity of a friendship by launching it into the choppy waters of a passionate relationship. In any case, apart from the Mills & Boon love stories of my early youth, I did fall in love again.

It was during the time of the Mahatma Gandhi University Youth Festival, where I was in charge of the makeup for the dances of Maharaja's College, Ernakulam. There was a wonderful energy in the air. It was crackling with the spirit of competition. All this was captured in the beautiful Malayalam film *Poomaram*, where I reprise my work as a makeup artist. The movie was a wonderful experience for me as it took me back to those days—to the excitement of that first meeting.

After applying the final touches to the dancers, I wandered around the performance area where the classical music competition was on. I don't remember anything about the singer; I don't think I even heard the song. But I still cannot forget the mridangam player who had been engaged to accompany the singer. He was so handsome that it took my breath away. I watched the performance in a haze and after it was done and he stepped down, I gathered my courage and said hello. He smiled and replied, and we chatted for a while. Finally, it was time for us to go our own ways, and he genially walked away, my heart trailing behind him. I suppose it was the universe conspiring, for I met him again at a classical dance performance organised by my mentor Sreenivas. This time we spent a lot of time getting to know each other and became good friends. That was enough for me. To have him in the circumference of my life was all I needed. And he was very considerate. He was the one who taught me how to save money. It was because of him that I opened a bank account, got a passbook and even a passport—things that I had never deemed essential. But he helped me understand my potential. And, in the process, I became indispensable for him. I had to be there by his side—the voice beside him assuring him of the emotional security he sought. There was absolute trust between us.

Then one day, he told me he was getting married. I was happy and hurt at the same time. Why had he not told me that he was going to meet a girl and he had liked her? I was happy because he would get a life partner who would give him the blessings of family life and the pleasures of intimacy that we had never engaged in. The love between us was unspoken. It was merely understood and so could be flatly denied at any point. Such is the fragility of love in my world! Anyway, I went along and was a part and parcel of the wedding arrangements. Even after he got married, we kept meeting. I would sometimes go to their home. I don't think his wife knew we were once a couple. I did not think it mattered either because apart from unspoken words and promises, there was nothing concrete that passed between us. He would hint at hypothetical situations like, 'It would be lovely if we could be together—if only the fates had ordained it.' Or, 'You are so wonderful. I know you will make a man very happy.'

He never ventured to say he was that man, and I never asked him outright if he wanted to be that man. Each time, I was felled by his cheeky smile. I became a family friend to his small family. In time, he had a daughter and I loved the child with all my heart. I still do. She loved me back. I think children are far more perceptive than we give them credit for. She could feel what I never revealed—my innate desire to be a mother. I invested my maternal instincts in her and she responded. I did not need anything or anyone else. This child was enough to make me happy.

Gradually, things began to become rather one-sided. I began to feel like I was being taken for granted, like a footstool or similar piece of furniture. I was expected to be at his beck and call. He would pretend or, well, I really don't know, he would make it seem like he could not function without me and insist on my proximity; after I arrived or the work was done, he would simply ignore me. The last straw was the time when his wife needed to travel to Thiruvananthapuram for a personal reason. He asked me to come along. My upcoming schedule was going to be really hectic and I told him as much. I needed my rest and there were arrangements to be made. But he would not take no for an answer. They both turned up, driver in tow, and picked me up. All through the journey of nearly 250 kilometres, we were talking and I was entertaining them with anecdotes from my film sets and so on. Once we reached our destination, he told me to check into a hotel and stay there or leave if I wanted to. I was shell-shocked and insulted. I came all the way on his whim and now he airily declares that I am free to go my way. It was of no concern to him that I was here on his invitation; no, I was made to come all that way while I had better things to do.

I decided that if my time could not be respected, then I did not want to have anything to do with him. And then the final rift happened. I realised he was embroiled in some unsavoury relationships and was not entirely honest in his marriage. He had crossed lines he never should have and had destroyed the sanctity of his marital vows. When I tried to reason with him, I was met with complete silence. This hurt me. I could not just stand there and see his life shattering and interact with his family as though nothing was happening. So, I gradually withdrew. I still think of his little one and how much she might have grown. Then I tell myself that those are oceans that I crossed a while ago, and now there is no turning my ship around.

He did call me many times after that, but I was polite and distant. I know that if I scratch around in the corners of my mind, I will still find vestiges of my infatuation. But I have long since put that torch out; only ashes remain. When I stopped all contact, I found myself at a loss—like I had suddenly been released onto a highway in the face of oncoming traffic. Then I corrected my course and made my withdrawal symptoms transformational. I threw myself into my work and began to work harder than ever.

Soon I became associated with JSR, a company that is a significant name in the fashion industry. I became their brand ambassador and launched my own salon and beauty academy, Dora Beauty World, in Aluva, Kerala. I started off small but, gradually, I incorporated best practices, innovated, made the space welcoming, brought it to world-class standards and made it one of the premier salons in the state. Soon there was talk of launching a branch in Kollam and that materialised as well. I started a branch in Dubai and now I spend my time between these three places when I am not on set or at an event. My salons bear the symbols of many religions. This is because I believe that all religions say the same thing and if we cannot accept diversity in religion, how will we accept diversity in human beings and in nature?

Thus I became an entrepreneur and teacher. Today, most transpersons who are working as makeup artists in Kerala have been trained by me. I keep two seats reserved for transpersons in every batch of my beautician training course. I handle most classes personally as the students have come to learn from me. They are women from many walks of life. There are those that are looking for a skill in their early forties and those who are in the first bloom of womanhood. For the duration of the course, at least, they are like a family. They are my family and, invariably, they take me under their wing, though I am their teacher. I am a strict teacher. I expect nothing but perfection and my mantra is, practice, practice, practice!

When it is lunch break, they bring their smiles out along with the food. Everyone gathers in a circle, opens their lunchboxes and talk with me. That is how I learn their stories and the struggles they face. In the course of the conversation, I walk around and they ask me to try some delicacy or the other; sometimes it's rice with sambar or fish curry or a *thoran*. I just have a mouthful, but it fills my stomach because it is given with such love and happiness. Lunch done, we go back to being teacher and students, and my voice fills the quiet classroom. I inevitably think of my life in a quick flashback during these sessions. I think, 'If only my brothers saw me now! The person they beat up so badly now is a teacher. She runs a business in two countries and has multiple residences.'

Speaking of residences, due to my frequent travels, I began to look for a home near Cochin International Airport. That is when an acquaintance offered his home on sale or on rent as per my choice. It is a wonderful, stately house that had everything I could ask for—adequate frontage, right near the main road and a hop and skip away from the airport. I moved right in. It was here, in this house, that my life took yet another interesting turn.

It was a sultry evening. I was out in the front yard, playing with my two dogs. I noticed two people walking by, craning their necks. As this sort of gawking happens quite often, I paid no heed. Then the two people walked back and stood at the gate. Now, this was unusual and irritating. I walked up to the gate. They were two young men. I asked them, '*Entha?*' (What is it?)

One of them grinned and said, 'We came to meet you, ma'am. He is a big fan and follows you on Instagram and watches your videos on YouTube as well.'

I was a bit mollified. I asked, 'Where do you stay? How did you know I live here?'

The young man who had been silent till then spoke up. 'I actually pass this way quite often. I have seen you come and go and also playing with your dogs on most evenings.'

'Oh?' I asked, 'don't you study or work then, if you have time to watch my activities?'

He looked abashed and his friend burst out laughing.

After that he would walk by on some evenings and call out a greeting or wave at me. One day he asked me if I would like to go on a walk with him. I agreed. It was after a very long time that I had gone out with someone. I wondered if it was alright to do that. We began walking in silence. Then he told me about himself and I too responded. We stopped for tea by the wayside and I was impressed by how unselfconscious he was. He was not looking around to see who was watching him drink tea with me, nor was he worried if anyone would say something provocative. We were just a man and a woman enjoying our tea.

I wanted to meet him more often. He began to drop by. We went on lunches and dinners, and I realised I was in love, plain and simple. While this was nothing new for me, the way I desired him was different. Perhaps it was because I was more confident in my body and its readiness to accept a man. I wanted him physically. I knew he too wanted to take the next step in our relationship. He stated that in very explicit words. I loved his candour. I loved that he did not want any ambiguity between us. For the first time, I desired to cross the very lines that I had drawn. There were intense debates in my mind—he had come to me, he wanted me, I had not hidden anything in this relationship and, above all, this body that I had created, that I had chosen and that the goddess had sanctified, had finally woken up to its needs and appetites. Why should I deny it something that is considered so natural? Why was I stubbornly denying my sexuality when I had embraced everything else about it?

These may sound like arguments of convenience, and they indeed are. The mind wants what it wants and so does the body. I knocked down the last of my defences and accepted him in a way I had never accepted anyone else. That coming together was everything I had hoped it would be. I saw desire and love in his eyes. I responded in kind. Contentment had a new definition for me. He took me home and introduced me to his parents as his celebrity friend. They were suitably impressed. I knew that to expect anything more was pointless, especially given the factors of age, social pressure and familial expectations. I wanted a child by surrogacy or adoption and he was not ready for such a commitment. There were things he wanted to accomplish, and entering into a serious, binding commitment like a marriage would be a big ask, especially given the level of visibility that being married to me would bring.

I nodded agreement to all the justifications he proffered and bid him a dignified goodbye. Closed the door. Perhaps this is the curse haunting every transperson, I thought—not finding fulfilment. Well, not everyone of us finds fulfilment. I do know perfectly happy couples—touchwood. Maybe I am not destined for that sort of happiness. I have celebrated the weddings of my daughters. They gave me the place of honour reserved for the mother of the bride. At the *mandapam* I have sometimes wondered if I too wanted a ceremony like this; if I wanted to sit beside someone who wanted to commit to me in front of the whole world. I have always suppressed these feelings. I don't think I want to be married at all. Companionship is what I look for—a comfortable companionship where there is perfect understanding, love and respect.

He went away, then returned after a while. We are friends now, or so I have told myself. When you have been denied all your life and have had to fight against every possible entity and agency to validate your own existence, then telling yourself to control your emotions is not a difficult thing. I see my life as a vehicle. People are welcome to hop on or off. I will not stop them, nor will I run after them. I think I am entitled to some guilty pleasure and then I return to my life and its rush and noise.

No one asked Chitrangada how she felt about her fate being already decided for her by her father and then, later, by the man she fell in love with. He of the broad shoulders and winning smile gave her a child, embraced her and walked away. Years later, after they met and he returned with her to Hastinapur, she took on the responsibility of caring for Gandhari. When the Pandavas made their final journey to the Himalayas, Chitrangada is said to have returned to her kingdom.

Am I to be Chitrangada—she who loved and lost, and lost yet again? Am I to love without inhibition and to take fatal decisions in the name of love? Be it mythology, drama or cinema, the Chitrangadas of this world search for closure.

Chapter Six

Renuka was Sage Jamadagni's wife. They had four sons. Renuka was of such pure character that she never had to carry a pot to collect water from the stream. She could simply fashion a pot from the sand of the riverbank and it would hold water. In some versions, the water would take the shape of the pot and follow her back to her home. But one day, she beheld some gandharvas sporting in the river with their lovers. This caused desire to rise within her. The mental infidelity caused her to lose strength of character and she could not fashion a pot of water. She was forced to return home and get a mud pot. Her husband, the hot-headed sage, noticed this and divined what had transpired. In a fit of rage, he approached each of his sons and demanded that they kill their mother for her transgression. Three of the boys refused to commit matricide. Jamadagni cursed them into oblivion, to live amongst people he perceived as 'lower-caste' and sub-human. The fourth boy was none other than Parasurama, the great sage. He took the clever route and agreed to kill his mother. He took her deep into the forest and cut her head off. The arc of the sword he swung also decapitated her maid, a woman from a 'lower caste', who was trying to save her.

Parasurama went back to the father, and Jamadagni was so pleased that he offered his son a boon of his choice. Immediately Parasurama asked that his mother be resurrected. Jamadagni knew he had been had, and reluctantly agreed to grant the boon, but attached a rider that only if the head was attached to the body before sundown would the boon work. Parasurama hurtled back to the forest and reached the spot just as the sun was setting. In his hurry, he transposed the body of his mother on the head of the maid and vice versa. They both sprung to life, fused together, and became Goddess Renuka-Yellamma. They asked the three sons to castrate themselves and become worshippers of the goddess so as to have a better life in the next birth. The sons did so and the goddess became the revered deity of transpersons.

In another part of the country is the legend of a horrendous and vicious dacoit who terrorised a number of villages. He attacks a caravan one night and assaults a young girl, who is the goddess incarnate. She assumes her true form and chases the dacoit. Just as he is about to die, he recognises his mistake and begs forgiveness. The goddess asks that he become her follower and he does so. That goddess is none other than Bahuchara Mata, who sits resplendent atop a rooster. She too is worshipped by transpersons as their mother.

A sense of anger at the injustice meted out to people and an ardent desire to restore the natural balance and harmony rests at the core of these divine figures who are worshipped by transpersons. These goddesses who watch over the poor, the disenfranchised, the cursed or the suffering—these are our mothers. It is to them that we transpeople entrust our life and our well-being.

***

Chapter Six 73

Some years ago, a young transperson wanted to have a gender affirmation surgery. She began earning from odd jobs and setting aside money. She lived in a lodge in a big city in Kerala. The money was kept well hidden in the room. Finally, she had enough money for her surgery. Her sister came to stay with her so she could go and do the preliminary checks. But the police raided the lodge as they suspected that there were illegal activities going on there. They took her money and took her as well. They beat her at the police station. When we at Dhwayah heard about this incident, I went to the station accompanied by a lawyer. The police admitted that they had no valid grounds for detaining this young person and were forced to release her. But the money had mysteriously disappeared. She had lost respect and her money as well. She did not look like she would be able to survive this humiliation. We stepped out of the police station and I saw the unspoken question in her eyes, 'Where will I go from here?' Fortunately, I already knew the answer.

We headed straight to the theatre workshop that was being conducted by the renowned dramatist Sreejith Master. I told the young person to pour out her story into a performance. She was a poet as well. She strung her suffering, humiliation, pain and sorrow into the most haunting melodies and sang them. This was how Daya Gayathri became part of the play *Parayaan Maranna Kathakal* (The Stories We Forgot to Tell).

One day, when I turned up for rehearsals, the girls were all full of naughty smiles and giggles. 'What is it?' I kept asking them. They chimed, 'Sreejith Master has an excellent role for you.' I imagined it must be the role of a bumbling or clumsy person or a comic relief because I keep saying funny things all the time. Sreejith Master narrated the role to me. I was taken aback. I told him that I did not think myself to be suitable for the role. It would jar, I said. He told me to give it a try.

It was the opening scene of the play. The stage is set in darkness. A transperson lights a lamp and incense sticks and prays to the goddess whose image is decked in flowers. And suddenly, the goddess springs to life. She is not the beauteous, serene figure you see in temples. She is Shakti incarnate. She holds in her hand a scimitar with bells attached. She has a belt of bells around her waist; her hair is in a loose braid; tendrils of hair fall on her face; the kohl in her eyes is smudged; her bindi is smeared. She is a terrible incarnation. She swirls onto the stage and takes her seat at the side, arms askew, legs akimbo, breathing heavily. From there she goes on to point out what ails humanity. She roars about the injustice meted out by parents, by the police, by the state, on transpersons. She asks if the transperson has no rights, if they are mere playthings for society to toy with and then cast aside.

Slowly, the stage fills up with transpeople who come forward to narrate their tales of woe and humiliation. The goddess blesses them all. She holds a mirror up to society which, while it is supposed to be made up of humans, is singularly lacking in humanity.

When Sreejith Master narrated this part, I was sure I would be an utter failure. So, I went ahead to perform the part to prove him wrong! But when I held the scimitar and roared for the first time, I don't know what came over me. I felt an energy course through me—a strange energy. It was like the goddess was there in the rehearsal space with us. I felt her flow in my veins. I said whatever I felt like instead of my allotted lines. The rehearsal was over before I could comprehend what was happening.

Sreejith Master told me, 'We will stick to the lines you said. They are better than the lines I gave you.' I was nonplussed. What did I say? Would I be able to recollect it?

I asked my teammates if they could repeat some of my lines so I could note them down and prepare. One of them said, 'Renjumma, leave it. Don't try to bring structure into your performance. Just keep doing what you are doing.'

I heeded those words. After that, I stopped trying to recall lines. The rehearsal space was often cathartic for most of us. There would such an outburst of emotions sometimes that we would all dissolve into tears. There were times when my teammates had to physically restrain me and calm me down, such was the energy I displayed in my performances.

The very first performance of *Parayaan Maranna Kathakal* brought the house down. We tasted success on every stage that we performed. And then the goddess in her infinite kindness brought us Revathiamma or A. Revathi, as you would know her. Activist, actor, author—you name it—A. Revathi has been there and done that. Her life story, *The Truth About Me: A Hijra Life Story*, is listed by Columbia University alongside the works of Maya Angelou and Toni Morrison as a great book that must be read. It was a happy chance that brought me into contact with her. We were sitting next to each other at an event and it was a fangirl moment for me. We got talking and soon exchanged numbers. One day, I happened to tell her about our play and the reception it had received and she was keen to watch it.

Not only did she watch it, she also agreed to become a part of the play in its subsequent performances. I remember that it was at All Saints' College, Thiruvananthapuram, that the play had its first performance featuring Revathiamma. We were back there after many years and yet again in front of an auditorium full of young girls and teachers. During the brief inaugural, when Revathiamma stood up to speak, the audience cheered loudly. One thing that she said stayed with me. She told the students, '*Sakkara venamnal oru paperile sakkara ennu eluthi pottaal athu inikaathu. Sakkarakku sakkara thaan venam*' (If you want sugar and you write the word 'sugar' on a piece of paper, it will not turn sweet. Where sugar is needed, you must have sugar.) She was talking about how legal rights and provisions and talk of giving respect, protection and livelihood opportunities to transpersons have forever remained just words. We needed actions, not just words—and we needed them yesterday.

The play unfolded; we had made modifications to it as time went by. This time, we incorporated representations of the wedding of Surya and Ishaan, the first transgender couple in Kerala to get married. They were there, both of them—the bride and groom—playing themselves, sitting on a decorated chair, while their families and their community stood around them, blessing them and celebrating their happy moments. In our community, such moments are few and far between; they are times of great happiness and joy. The audience also celebrated with us. Soon, the stage turned dark and ominous and the keeper of the burning *ghats*, played by Revathiamma, took over. She talked of murder, death and violence, and the stage suddenly turned violent simply through her words.

She spoke viscerally of the ways in which transpersons are violated, harassed and killed, but no one is held accountable. Her voice was heavy with the weight of her knowledge of innumerable such cases.

We also showed the students our talents in dance, fashion designing and ramp walking, and literally brought the house down. We were given a standing ovation; and despite it being far beyond their lunchtime, no student left the hall! It was such a carnival and we all enjoyed ourselves.

Revathiamma went on to perform at many stages with us. She is a great mentor and friend. And together, the two of us women end up doing all sorts of zany things. I call her *chinna ponnu* or little girl. When she comes to stay, I braid her hair and cook for her, and sometimes she makes something delicious for me as well. It is a friendship that we have grown to cherish and love. It is my island of stability amid the roiling ocean that sometimes is my life. I know that there are great things in store for this friendship, and for what we wish to do for our community.

***

I am sometimes amazed that I have lived to tell this tale. And I continue to be surprised that I am still standing and indeed walking forward. Someone once told me that the trick of getting ahead in life is to place one foot in front of the other and that before you know it, you will have reached your destination. What is my destination? I have only a vague idea and lots of dreams and hopes. While I initially walked towards them, now I have started driving towards them! I recently got my driver's licence. And I try to drive whenever and wherever I can. My favourite vehicle is my Thar. I feel a sense of power when I drive it. Sometimes my daughters and I drive out at night and park by the wall along the airport runway. It is beautiful at night—the lit runway, the flights landing and taking off, the immense power that lifts all that weight into the air, and then the plane looks light as a feather, sailing serenely through the night sky. Seeing these planes, with their lights flashing in the sky, fills me with a sense of peace. I can sit for hours in my car, watching this unfold as though it is the most natural thing in the world. There are occasional cups of tea as well that go with all this gazing.

I eventually wind up thinking that humans have progressed so much, made so much possible, performed medical and scientific miracles, made tonnes of metal, flown across the globe and all the way to space, landed on the moon, probed Mars, and yet—and yet consider transpeople unnatural. Society considers love between consenting adults unnatural. Parents who nurture their children with their life-blood reject them in one fell swoop, or send them to conversion therapy when the child wants to present themselves as different from the 'normal'. It is indeed strange. When I look around at the members of my community, I see so many people who could have had such promising careers, done so much better in life, had they not been forced to fend for themselves at such a young age. When children are hungry and disowned, survival is the only thing at the top of their minds. Alone and with no one to guide them, they have to do what they can to live from day to day.

And then? When they are twenty-five or thirty years of age, we set out to educate, upskill and teach them that there are greater things in life than hunger and a roof above their heads. Will all those who pontificate about transpersons not sticking to jobs they are provided with—even if they are low-paying jobs that don't even cover rent, and if they do find accommodation, they are charged double the normal rent and viewed with suspicion all the time—go hungry for two days and survive on the streets with nothing but tap water and garbage? The new laws that have been passed for the protection of transpersons are good, but are also problematic.

The Transgender Persons (Protection of Rights) Act, 2019 allows for self-perceived gender identity. There are provisions against discrimination in education, employment, healthcare and living spaces, and it has been made mandatory that there be a National Council for Transgender Persons which must address the issues of transpeople of the country. However, fundamental problems still remain—mainly that of policy and implementation. While we are allowed to self-determine our identity, there is a need for it to be certified by a district magistrate; and once the gender affirmation surgery has taken place, one must submit oneself before a medical board. What of the autonomy of the individual? This opens up the possibility of red tape, corruption and mental distress for the transperson.

The Act insists that a minor identifying as a transperson has every right to stay in their house with their family. But think about the hostility the child faces, the emotional blackmail, the possibility of violence—both physical and sexual. In the face of relentless assault, how much longer can a child hold on? And, most importantly, what would be the mental state of a child living under such stress? Who is to answer to that? There is also the problem of skewed focus, that as transwomen are more visible, there is little focus on transmen, intersex and gender-queer persons. The diversity that we would like to see in society is not reflected even on paper.

The good fight is still not over. We have miles to go before we can sleep. I strongly believe that we must band together and create our own destinies. We must create a circular economy that can generate immense benefits for our communities. That is one of the surest ways of achieving legal and social recognition in India. We are brilliant people, we are administrators, professionals, entertainers, entrepreneurs—we are a micro-economy in and of ourselves. Why don't we look for self-reliance and make ourselves heard and not just seen?

And let us be heard and seen as economically, socially, politically and culturally compelling citizens. Our community has roots across the globe. Let us use that to create a great renaissance. When money and agency speak, the world listens. This is the way forward in this world.

I have a dream of a university of cosmetology, a residential one. There will be students from all stations of life there. It will be not only for learning how to apply makeup professionally, but also for teaching dermatology and cosmetic procedures, both basic and advanced. Maybe it is a far-fetched dream. But everything starts with a dream, right? It was beyond the wildest of dreams that the biologically male child of Thankappan and Thankamma, who had themselves never crossed the borders of their state, would one day travel the world, and that too as a woman! Yet here I am. I don't know what the future holds for me. I was someone very different at the start of this narrative and as it concludes, I have become someone else altogether. This is life. You change, you transform. Some transformations are more painful, complete, complex and visible than others. It is good to change. I wish you all marvellous changes in your lives—changes for the better!

***

Just one thing—I know many people have wondered about my name. I was not born Renju Renjimar. Those were the heady days of Facebook. I was just learning the ropes of social media. To sign up, one had to provide a name and a surname. In my mind, I had given up my birth name a while ago. So, my friend suggested I use the name I chose for myself. I typed in 'Renju'. Then there was the surname, so I typed in 'Renjima'—a variation of Renjumma—the name my friends fondly called me. The 'r' in 'Renjimar' was actually a typo! Thus I got my name, a combination of a choice, some love and a misstep. Like Renuka-Yellamma. Some confusion and a fusion.

My name is just like my life. My name *is* my life. It all starts with a name, no?

Chapter Seven

It is said there was once a king named Sikhidhwaja who was married to Chudala. They both receive lessons in spiritual attainments. The queen comes to a spiritual realisation faster than the king. This does not make him happy and he attributes the reason for his lack of progress to his royal responsibilities. He leaves his kingdom under Chudala's charge and decides to retreat into the forest to live the life of an ascetic. Chudala tries to makes him understand that merely shunning his worldly responsibilities does not make him spiritually accomplished and that he has to learn to let go of his sense of self. But he ignores her ideas on the grounds that she is a mere woman. So Chudala, who has the power of shape-shifting, appears before Sikhidhwaja in the forest in the guise of a man, Kumbha, and befriends him. Sikhidhwaja appreciates Kumbha's inputs and respects his views. They pass their days in deep dialogues and discourse. However, Kumbha/Chudala finds that Sikhidhwaja is unable to understand that spirituality should not be considered gendered and that the self must be transcended for true realisation.

Kumbha tells Sikhidhwaja, 'As I teased him while he was hurrying along, I have been cursed by Sage Durvasa—to transform into a woman each night. So, I will be a woman while I share your bed at night.' Shikhidhwaja does not raise any objections and shares his bed dispassionately and detachedly. Soon Kumbha requests that they be intimate as he wants to understand how a woman experiences pleasure. He tells Sikhidhwaja that he would not lose his celibacy as the act would not be amorous. So, Sikhidhwaja obliges. They are duly married and consummate the relationship as well. Kumbha becomes Madanika at night and the couple spends time with each other. But Madanika can feel that Sikhidhwaja is quite detached. She then decides to test him further. She creates an enchantment where he sees Indra sporting with the apsaras while maintaining a sense of detachment. Next, she creates an illusion where she is being intimate with a stranger. When Sikhidhwaja sees them together, he walks out of the room. Soon, Madanika joins him, looking embarrassed at being discovered. But Sikhidhwaja does not chastise her. Instead, he tells her it was unnecessary to have come away so soon and to bask a while longer in her lover's embrace. Madanika/Kumbha/Chudala then tells him that he has truly mastered the self as he is able to view life without any sense of possessiveness. When someone is truly able to let go, they have attained enlightenment and are really free. Chudala reveals her true self and it is then that Sikhidhwaja understands the folly of rejecting Chudala's wisdom on the grounds of her being a woman. They return to their kingdom and, I imagine, live happily ever after.

It is this detachment that I am looking for in life. Becoming an ascetic is still beyond me. I am enjoying my creature comforts. But there is a gnawing sense of sadness within me that I have been trying to overcome. It is a heady, dizzying sense of euphoria when a relationship starts off, isn't it? You recall those sidelong glances, the giggles, the surreptitious way that your fingers brush in public, the daring feeling you get when you put your arms around each other in public when you think no one is watching, or just because someone is watching with too keen an interest. Then things settle into a beautiful rhythm. You complete each other's sentences; any visit to a shop becomes a reason to buy him something. Everything becomes a context to think of him. Sometimes, I marvel at the person I suddenly become. I used to warn my daughters, 'Di, don't go falling head over heels in love. Remember, when the money runs out, so will he. Keep a portion of your mind for yourself. Don't give him your all.' None of them listened to me. They still don't in this regard. And then I found that even I was not obeying my own instructions. Like a kite caught in the high winds, my heart just took off, soared and soared.

Then I found that I could not land. The winds had died; the sky was empty; my heart did not know how to descend. It kept lingering in the hope that there would be a current coming to save it—but no. The demise of a relationship is very easy to gauge. It is when one of the couple starts to behave in a shifty way. There is no real joy in receiving gifts; there is a sense of tiredness in the responses. It is the responses that gave me my first clue about my beloved neighbour who had pursued me so earnestly. Earlier, I would send long messages and get equally long messages back, adoring expressions of love and a lot of endearments. Towards the end, there would be just a *hmm* or an *okay* or a thumbs-up as response. I found it humiliating. Like I was not a human being with feelings. I wondered if he thought I was not human, that I could just be fobbed off without even the decency of an explanation. Those were dark days for me.

The various treatments that I was undergoing after the surgery, especially the hormone treatment, were making me put on weight. There were certain clothes I wanted to wear, but I often had to think twice because of my weight concerns. And then there was the sorrow of having been cast aside like this. I really did not know whom to turn to or what to do. At one point, everything seemed even more desolate. I went through a crisis of self-worth. I wondered if it was time to end it all.

While contemplating death, I fell into a state of deep sleep. And what I dreamt were scenes from my life from an earlier time.

There I was, dressed as a man, sitting outside a tea stall, talking to people. I was holding a glass of tea and someone cracked a joke. I laughed and it came out high-pitched; I sounded like a woman. Which I was—for me—but not for the men sitting around me. Suddenly one of the men slapped the side of my head. I did not even know him. 'Da! Laugh like a man. What is this sound coming out of you?' This was followed by some more knocks on the head by random guys. It was like suddenly everyone had the license to express an opinion and they could do so while laying their hands on me. There were times when, walking down the road, I would be singing to myself or lost in thought, and my hips might sway or my hand might lift in a feminine way. The dirty looks I received from random strangers would have crushed the confidence of someone less resilient. One day, I was simply walking along the road when I swayed a little, and suddenly felt a kick in my back. I stumbled and fell hard onto the roadside. When I looked up, an auto-driver was glaring at me with pure hostility before speeding away—apparently satisfied that he had just *rescued* masculinity from the likes of me. What could I have done in this situation? I got up, looked at the scrapes on my arms and knees and cursed the man in my mind. Then I got up and walked on, knowing all the while that there were people staring curiously at me, wondering about me. I knew they would probably go home and sneer at the effeminate fool who was shown his place by a culture-abiding man or, possibly, they would forget all about me. I would probably be not even as memorable as a dead cat or dog by the road.

Chapter Seven

I survived this casual cruelty.

I had no formal training in makeup. But I learnt. I learnt the art of reading the face. I learnt how to understand the flaws in the skin and the face and how to rectify them. I learnt about the science of the skin—its structure and anatomy. I learnt—through my own intelligence, keen observation, constant trial and error, and hours of painstaking handiwork—to alter the angles of the face and highlight features so that everything else recedes into the background. I learnt to use technology, and to discern between the necessary and the flashy. I learnt to assess products, understand quality, render services, and read the needs of the times. I earned trust—one brushstroke, one contour shape at a time.

I survived prejudice.

I understood that to stand still, to repeat oneself, is to die. So, I keep diversifying, I keep innovating. I did not just remain a travelling celebrity makeup artist. I decided to put down roots. I opened one salon which then became three in India. I dared to dream big. Dubai had always been my dream city. I have always felt a sense of security there that I have rarely felt anywhere else. 'Do I dare open a salon in Dubai?' I asked myself. 'Why not?' came the answer from the depths of my mind. 'We have nothing to lose!' And so, it happened. The universe conspired to make it happen. One became two and then became three. I also have a place to stay in Dubai. My salons carry my picture in the display area facing the street; sometimes I see people standing there looking at my larger-than-life photo and I feel a sense of pride and achievement that I cannot begin to describe. If I go walking by, sometimes people stop me and ask, 'Hey, isn't this you?', and they chat and tell me they are very happy to see my rise. I form a kinship with these people who are simply happy to have met me, who take a selfie with me and walk away. I feel proud during such moments.

I survived insecurity.

My house that I spoke of earlier was a small structure with a thatched roof and walls made of mud. Every year when it rained my parents would look at each other anxiously. They tried to hide their worry, but we children knew it was time to slowly pack our things and move to the school that we studied in. The school would turn into a relief camp during the monsoons for poor families like ours. It felt odd and sad that the school we studied in became a camp where we lived for weeks. The classrooms would take on a different aspect, a different purpose. It was difficult to adjust to such wildly fluctuating realities. After the rains and when the floods had receded we would go back, hoping for the best but fearing the worst. Sometimes our house would have survived the damage, but more often than not, we would have to start from scratch. With the passage of time, the structure was rebuilt with more durable materials, and the roof was replaced with a more lasting one. But still, we had to move out when it rained. After decades—now—there stands a pucca house on a higher level: a two-storeyed house that I built.

I survived crushing poverty.

I've had barely any higher education to speak of. I wanted to study but the realities of who I am clashed with the expectations of what others wanted me to be. I could no longer sustain the charade, and when I left home, my education ended as well. I was promised opportunities, but nothing came of them. No one really bothered to keep their promises. In Kochi, I would buy soda from the stalls outside St Teresa's College and watch the girls stream in and out of the campus. That was all I could do. But when I clawed my way to survival, I ended up entering that college as a hired makeup artist for their programmes and then as a guest for an event, and then as a student in their classes in communicative English. Finally, when the NAAC (National Assessment and Accreditation Council) peer team visited the college for assessment and accreditation, the college invited me as their guest to interact with the peer team. I, who had no formal education, sat before eminent educationists and spoke about education and the change it can bring in. Now, I take courses offered by the University of London in Dubai. I am gaining qualifications that were out of reach for me at one point. I am invited to speak to students about gender. I teach students at my academy. The place where my salon and academy now stand in Kollam was once a spot where I was harassed and insulted. I held the inauguration of my salon in that very place, and I was able to invite my mother to do the honours. Her presence meant more to me than all the film stars who came to celebrate with me that day. Today, no matter what time of day or night I arrive in my hometown, there are always dozens of people who come up to talk to me, ask if I need anything, or offer to drop me home. It is nothing but love they have for me. I have come a long way from being stomped on or being insulted. I have reinvented myself.

I survived the limitations of social imagination.

I opened my eyes and sat up ramrod-straight. I realised how close I had come to not wanting to live anymore—how dangerously close I was to believing that this one loss was all that mattered, and to defining myself entirely through that single relationship. I realised that I had become the very person I had always warned my daughters and friends not to become. I had become weak and had veered away from my purpose. I suddenly felt ashamed of myself. In the middle of the night, I sat on my bed and looked at my hands in the pitch-black darkness of my bedroom. I could not see them, but I knew they were there—that I was holding them before my face. I asked myself, 'Who are you? Who did you want to become and what have you become?'

Suddenly, I felt the room go cold. I was transported to the stage of *Parayaan Maranna Kathakal*; the Devi swirled like a dervish and laughed maniacally. She kept asking this question over and over again. When I came to my senses, I was shivering though I was drenched in sweat. I had not moved from the bed. I understood that for this relationship, I had chained and caged my inner strength. Now as I was standing on the precipice preparing to jump off, it had broken free and had come to save me. I surrendered to that higher power. I swore that I would not let myself become vulnerable again. Realising the self and harnessing it is the greatest form of power. I was ready to embrace myself yet again. I was ready to live.

And now I am living—to the fullest. I work hard, I enjoy myself. I do not hold back on the things I need because I feel I have earned them. These days, there is very little I covet or feel the need for. And when I do want something, I simply get it—because I now live in a way that, even if death were to call me, I would be ready to go with it like an old friend. And yes, death is indeed an old friend. I have died so many deaths that life itself seems like an interlude between two deaths.

***

People who know me ask me if I feel like I have won a hard-fought battle. I maintain that this is life. It is my life. That is all it is. There is no victory or defeat. There is only life. It might sound sanctimonious, but I feel that we simply move from one situation to the next. I am responsible for my joys and sorrows. No one else can be held responsible. They are *my* joys, *my* sorrows; and the red flags I had to live with were also *my* decisions. The need for a drastic change was also *my* decision. There are no battles here. Just a poor soul with a handful of dreams—dreams she has often had to crush, and then smile through the pain.

I want my life to matter—to mean something. Not because I want a monument erected in my name. No. It is because I want my community to know that we count. I want them to stand up and be counted, too. I have trained my daughters in the art of makeup. I have ensured that they get opportunities that I had to carve out for myself. It is the least I can do. All those who have trained under me now have careers of their own as makeup artists. I want society to understand that there is more to us than the stereotypes it has laid out for us. When my daughters step out of their homes with their makeup products and send me pictures of their work, I feel proud. Life feels good. My academies are also places where women form communities of love and trust. Sometimes they open up to me. The other day, I was in the lobby when a young woman walked in to enrol for a course. There was something in her voice—part defensiveness, part apprehension. I understood that she was coming from a place of trauma. I gently asked her if she was okay. She drew a shaky breath and told me that this was the first big step she had taken in her life in a very long time. She had been married off quite early and had been subjected to cruelty by her husband. She had led a life of deprivation and abuse and when she could not take it anymore, she left. She saw this course at my academy as her ticket to freedom and financial security. Hence she came to join us. I was very happy listening to this account. I was thankful that she had not succumbed to impulses of self-harm and had instead chosen to be proactive.

This is the sort of resilience that human beings must show. I am incredibly proud to have mentored a number of such women who were seeking a way out of their miserable situations. The idea is to never give up. As I have mentioned before, I have built a house in Kollam as a tribute to my old home. It is there that my family gathers when there is a family function. It is also where anyone from my community is welcome to stay. And they do stay there sometimes when I am at home. We laugh, cook, and create a little world of our own. It feels as if no one else exists in the whole world. The house has a large courtyard with a lovely tree in one corner. On the other side are the kennels for the dogs. My little Koosi sometimes stays there too.

When I was going through the pangs of the breakup, I had scant regard or respect for my life. But when I looked around me, I realised that a lot of people depended on me. I don't just mean my community or my employees or my students—also my immediate family. They are quite dependent on me. If something happened to me, what would they do? Thus, rather than be where I was not wanted, I decided to be where I was needed—my home, my academy, my community and with my mother.

My mother has grown old. Her eyes have become weak. But her memory is still sharp. She remembers everything about the past, and interviewers often seek her out for a sound bite. She always obliges and never disappoints. Each time she speaks she recounts some incident from my past. It makes me understand how much she loves me and how hard it must have been for her when I went away from home after being traumatised by my brothers. When I returned home after many years, my voice had changed and I had gradually transitioned. My mother cared only that I had returned—never about who I was or what I had become. It is society that creates such anxieties. But nothing of that sort can ever stand in the way of an Indian mother and her son or daughter. My mother still maintains that I returned to her on account of the many prayers she had offered to the many deities, all of whom she is grateful to even today.

My mother is sensitive to any changes in my temperament or routine. As I mentioned earlier, I was putting on weight, and it became important to lose it for health reasons. I began surviving on very little food. At first, my mother did not say anything, and I let myself slip into a false sense of security. But suddenly, she went into full guerrilla mode, insisting that I take second helpings of everything. She told me, 'I have already lost a daughter. What will I do without you?' I looked at my mother. Her eyes, dimmed with age, were brimming with tears. I realised that she does not think of me as her son—not even in passing.

I looked around my house and saw my family gathering around the evening lamp I had lit earlier. There were generations standing there. I knew I had to live for them. Even if no one on this earth wants me, they do. They depend on me. It is not just financial dependency I am talking about; it is also their sense of emotional security. It is a rather depleted family that I hold close now. My father, brother and sister are no longer here. I have come to terms with the loss of my father. He was bedridden for five years. No one from my family turned up to help with the expenses. But I did not mind. I bore all the expenses. I single-handedly took care of all his medical needs. I would buy all the medicines and supplies and take them home. I was not a big name or anything remarkable back then, but I managed. I gave my father the dignity of never having to worry about his own care, and for the first time, I felt my life had meaning.

My brother who had tormented me and led me to leave home, became a quiet, reserved figure after I returned. I don't think I have fully processed those emotions yet. We eventually lost him to complications related to alcohol abuse. My sister was my favourite after my mother. I loved her wholeheartedly and she loved me too. We used to be a team. She was the one who witnessed all my wild behaviour, and she endured all my early attempts at femininity. I see her children as mine. In fact, I consider all my siblings' children as mine; I am there for them however I can.

It was the midnight of 23 September 2023, and I had just returned home from work. I knew my sister was not feeling well, so I went upstairs to check on her. She had a raging fever, but she was conscious. I wanted to take her to the doctor immediately. Initially, she resisted, but soon gave in and walked to the car despite our entreaties. Then she turned back to the house to fetch money for the hospital, even though I kept telling her I had enough with me. At the hospital, she was admitted; the diagnosis was pneumonia. She passed away quietly. My wonderful, uncomplaining sister who had, in a sense, brought us all up, had gone. I felt bereft. I think I still mourn her. Now there are just the two of us left among our parents' children—my brother and I.

***

I was told that my niece, my sister's daughter, has come of age. In our part of the world, it is a matter of great happiness and is celebrated. In the morning, a soft knock sounded on the door. When I opened it, my niece was standing there. Standing shyly behind her was her friend. The two came into the room. My little one proudly introduced her friend to me. I smiled at both of them. Then her friend gestured to my niece. She looked sheepish. I understood. Still, I pretended to not notice and asked them, 'How would you like me to dress you up for the occasion?' The girls clapped their hands in delight. Though I had dressed my girl many times for fun, this was the first time I was doing it for a formal occasion—one that marked a significant turning point in her life.

'Okay, so sit very still,' I told her. Out of the corner of my eye, I could see her friend also sitting still, holding her breath so that I was not disturbed. I began by outlining the almond-shaped eyes of my child. With just a smidgeon of foundation, I enhanced her duskiness and brought out the highlights of her face. With a couple of brushstrokes, I finished her makeup. Looking back at me was a young woman on the threshold of womanhood and the attendant storms it will bring. I saw the hopes, dreams, aspirations, doubts and trepidation that I once felt. I am glad my niece has one less thing to worry about in this world. She is perfect in her own skin—unlike me, who had to spend years sculpting my body and my identity. I held up the mirror. Her eyes widened in surprise and excitement. It made me immensely happy. I applied makeup on her friend too and they both went bouncing down the stairs.

When I went down, wearing my favourite Kerala saree, they were all waiting for me—my family. My mother offered her prayers, and I asked her to give the first auspicious token for a healthy, fertile life. My mother held out her offering with both hands. I looked at those hands—so frail, so fragile. It was hard to believe that these were the same hands that once shelled hot cashew nuts and even beat up nine policemen for helping open a liquor store in our hometown. She proudly proclaims that, till date, our native place, Pundalathalam, has not had a single liquor store. Neighbouring localities may have liquor stores, but not our area. In her youth, my mother was a political activist and also a staunch supporter of people's rights. I suppose four children must have taken their toll on her body. The pressures of the life she had led were etched deep in her palms. The firebrand had not calmed down though. I still see the spark when she speaks to reporters or people who come to seek her advice. My mother gave my niece her blessings. I too closed my eyes in gratitude, thankful to have all of them close to me. I know that these are also the people I must live for. I want to see my niece grow up and become a woman of substance. I want to see her sail confidently into the world and try and make it a better place. I want her to spread the message of acceptance and kindness.

My mother's older sister did not have children for a long time. Out of her heart's desire, she would buy clothes meant for children and stock them in her cupboard in the hope that one day she would be able to dress her children in those clothes. I was the cynosure of her eyes. She would insist on dressing me in the clothes she had bought for her future son. It annoyed me to no end, though I was not yet five. One day, as she was getting me ready for the temple—the very same temple I mentioned at the beginning of this narrative—I began howling for a frock from the cupboard. Despite her best attempts, I refused to back down. Giving up, she dressed me in the frock. At the entrance to the sanctum sanctorum, I suddenly felt the urge to pee and, not knowing any better, I simply did so. The people nearby were horrified. But the story that outlived the moment—almost a local myth for days—was that a girl had come to the Devi's door and been turned into a boy!

Since then, my life has been a miracle.

Sonya J. Nair is the Head of the Department of English at All Saints' College, Thiruvananthapuram, Kerala. She is the editor of *samyuktapoetry.com* and is currently working on a monograph on transgender festivals in South India.